MINIMALIST LIFESTYLE

How to Become a Minimalist, Declutter Your Life and Develop Minimalism Habits & Mindsets to Worry Less and Live More

By
Jenifer Scott

© Copyright 2019 by Jenifer Scott - All rights reserved.

This book is provided with the sole purpose of providing relevant information on a specific topic for which every reasonable effort has been made to ensure that it is both accurate and reasonable. Nevertheless, by purchasing this book you consent to the fact that the author, as well as the publisher, are in no way experts on the topics contained herein, regardless of any claims as such that may be made within. As such, any suggestions or recommendations that are made within are done so purely for entertainment value. It is recommended that you always consult a professional prior to undertaking any of the advice or techniques discussed within.

This is a legally binding declaration that is considered both valid and fair by both the Committee of Publishers Association and the American Bar Association and should be considered as legally binding within the United States.

The reproduction, transmission, and duplication of any of the content found herein, including any specific or extended information will be done as an illegal act regardless of the end form the information ultimately takes. This includes copied versions of the work both physical, digital and audio unless express consent of the Publisher is provided beforehand. Any additional rights reserved.

Furthermore, the information that can be found within the pages described forthwith shall be considered both accurate and truthful when it comes to freely available information and general consent. As such, any use, correct or incorrect, of the provided information will render the Publisher free of responsibility as to the actions taken outside of their direct purview. Regardless, there are zero scenarios where the original author or the Publisher can be deemed liable in any fashion for any damages or hardships that may result from any of the information discussed within.

Finally, any of the content found within is ultimately intended for entertainment purposes and should be thought of and acted on as such. Due to its inherently ephemeral nature nothing discussed within should be taken as an assurance of quality, even when the words and deeds described herein indicated otherwise. Trademarks and copyrights mentioned within are done for informational purposes in line with fair use and should not be seen as an endorsement from the copyright or trademark holder.

TABLE OF CONTENTS

Introduction 1

CHAPTER 1 *Hello, New Minimalist You* 2

CHAPTER 2 *What's Life Like As A Minimalist Anyway?* 10

CHAPTER 3 *Where It All Begins* 18

CHAPTER 4 *The Rulebook To Living With Less* 26

CHAPTER 5 *Can I Minimize Other Areas Too?* 34

CHAPTER 6 *Shifting Your Mindset* 41

CHAPTER 7 *Goal Setting* 49

CHAPTER 8 *Success Tips For Your New Way Of Life* 57

Description 67

INTRODUCTION

Congratulations on purchasing this book and thank you for doing so. You've picked up this book for a reason.

That reason is that you are ready to make a change in your life. You're ready to be free of what's weighing you down. Free from the home that is full of unused items taking up space that you can't stand to see the mess any longer. Free from the urge to constantly keep buying, buying, buying and feeling like it's never enough.

That change is about to take place now, a change for the better, a change for a completely new way of living. Welcome, to the minimalist lifestyle.

Minimalism may seem to be a new concept to you as you're just starting out on this process, but this concept has actually existed for a long time. Evidence of this lifestyle is seen almost throughout Japan, and in the Western world, several prominent individuals are already reaping the benefits of minimalism and experiencing the joy of living with less. The reason why this concept is growing in popularity and gaining more traction in recent times is that people are starting to wake up to the fact that materialism does not equate to happiness. That filling your life with the latest gadgets, fashion trends, furniture or trinkets is not going to bring you the happiness that you seek.

People are starting to wake up to the fact that *true happiness* has been right in front of them all along, in the things that matter most, which are relationships, health, love and all the other things that cost you nothing. These are the things that were forgotten along the way as the consumerist lifestyle slowly took over (and continues to take over). Constantly being exposed to ad after ad, always encouraging us to buy more, subliminal messages telling us we won't be 'happy' or 'complete' until we have this or that has gone on for far too long.

It is now time to get connected once again with the little things in life that matter. The values that you hold most dear. It is time to reconnect with the true things that bring happiness, and it starts right here with decluttering your life and making way for a new life as a minimalist.

There are plenty of books on this subject on the market, thanks again for choosing this one! Every effort was made to ensure it is full of as much useful information as possible. Please enjoy!

CHAPTER 1
Hello, New Minimalist You

When was the last time you took a good, long, hard look at your life? All the material possessions you have accumulated around your home. Have you ever looked at your surroundings and thought to yourself, *how on earth did I accumulate SO much stuff?* Not to mention the amount of money you have spent buying a lot of stuff which you don't need (yikes! Let's not go down that path just yet). If you're tired of seeing the mess and clutter that surrounds your home, and maybe even several other aspects of your life, then it's high time to do something about it.

You are about to embark on a journey that is about to change your life in ways you couldn't previously imagine. The liberation, the freedom that you're going to feel, not to mention how much *lighter* everything is going to seem when you declutter some of the mess you may have gathered over the years is going to feel like a weight off your shoulders. You are about to venture into the world of minimalist living.

Wait, What? What Is Minimalism?

While this may be a concept which has been gaining popularity in the western world, minimalism is actually a practice which has been around for a long time. The Japanese are prime examples of people who have mastered the art of minimalist living, and the rest of the world is now catching up because we are finally starting to realize just how beneficial this kind of lifestyle can be.

Have you ever been to Japan? If you haven't a quick Google or Pinterest search will reveal how the Japanese live in small, confined spaces with very minimal possessions within this environment. Their homes may be small, yet it doesn't look cluttered and claustrophobic.

But first, what is minimalism? Joshua Fields Millburn and Ryan Nicodemus, authors of *Minimalism: Live a Meaningful Life* defined minimalism as *"a tool to rid yourself of life's excess for focusing on what's important so that you can find happiness, fulfilment and freedom."* That certainly sounds promising, especially when we're all in pursuit of happiness in one way or another. Nobody ever wants to be unhappy, and while we know that we need to work on happiness internally, we also need to work on it externally, which means creating an environment around us that helps us *focus* on what's important in our lives. Minimalism, according to Millburn and Nicodemus, is an approach that can help with this.

A minimalist lifestyle is meant to teach us that we do not have to turn to material things to find comfort and happiness in our lives. That *we can be happy* even without having these material possessions around us. We don't always need the latest gadgets, the latest fashion trends, or even the latest car models to keep us happy. That happiness, as cliché as it sounds, does come from within after all. We can find happiness in the company of our family and friends. We can find happiness in our pets, find happiness is pursuing the activities that we love, watching a favorite movie at the end of a long day, perhaps even happiness in the careers that we embark on. Happiness is a subjective concept and living a minimalist lifestyle is going to help you connect with what it means *for you* to be happy again.

Just to be clear, there is nothing *wrong* with owning material possessions. Not at all. Living a minimalist life is simply living with *only what you need* to keep you fulfilled and happy. Nothing more. You are still going to have stuff in your life and your home. You're just not going to have *so much* of it, that's the difference. We have become far too consumeristic and materialistic, and it is time to change all of that. In the pursuit of keeping up with this constant, on-the-go and hectic lifestyle, we have forgotten that there are other aspects of our life which need looking after. Our health, relationships, personal growth and mental health have taken a backseat as we race for what else we can buy, who has what new item and finding reasons to constantly make new and unnecessary purchases we don't need.

Does Minimalist Living Come with Benefits? Why Should I Do This?

Yes, it does, which is why this concept is quickly gaining traction and popularity. As human beings, we're wired to be motivated to make a change for the better if we know that there is some benefit in it for us.

Understandably, the thought of getting rid of most of what you have accumulated over the years can be a daunting thought. Some people have a very strong emotional attachment to certain possessions that they own, even if they may not have used or touched those items in years. Yet, they find it difficult to part with these items. *What if I may need it one day? I could possibly use it again. There may be an occasion where I'm going to need this, so maybe I better hold on to it. I can't get rid of this; it's special to me.* Those are just some of the thoughts that run through a person's mind when they think about whether or not they just keep or toss an item.

The benefits of living minimalist, however, is far more than the physical changes that you see happening around your environment. These are changes that you experience are also going to be felt from within, and those are the changes which are more powerful than anything that takes place in your external surroundings. Minimalism brings you right back to what matters the most by reminding you that you don't need to constantly rely on materialistic belongings to feel like a fulfilled and happy individual. The benefits that you are going to feel and see happening within and around you include:

- **You Will Become More Motivated** - With a clear purpose in your life and without the unnecessary distractions taking away

your focus, you will once more be able to see your purpose and what you want to accomplish in your life.
- **Your Mental Health Improves** - When you once more begin to focus on yourself, it reminds you of what you have been neglecting all along. That *you matter more* than any material possessions you could possibly buy, and when you start to focus on yourself again, your mental and physical health starts to shine because you're working on becoming a better you.
- **You Will Feel A Sense of Relief** - Clearing away the clutter in your life is going to feel like a big weight has been lifted off your shoulders. Suddenly, you have room to breathe again once more. We often don't realize just how much we are affected by the clutter and accumulation of possessions around us until we get rid of it and feel much better when we've tossed out a few items.
- **You Are Teaching Yourself A Valuable Life Lesson** - Believe it or not, you'll be teaching yourself a valuable life lesson when you start seeing those material possessions are not responsible for bringing you happiness. Living as a minimalist is going to remind you every single day to be happy and grateful for the things that you already possess in your lives, and that if something is not necessary for your survival, then you probably don't need it after all.
- **Your Relationships Improve** - When you learn to be happy with what you have instead of constantly competing with everyone around you, your relationships with the people who matter most especially will start to improve for the better. The need to feel jealous over a friend or family member who has the latest car or smartphone model, or perhaps even purchase a new home or a new clothing item no longer exists, because you have no room in your life for trivial things that don't really matter.
- **There's Now Time To Be More Efficient** - You are able to concentrate better, your priorities more in focus, you find yourself feeling lighter, happier, and able to work a lot more efficiently and make more productive use of your time because you have fewer things around you that distract you.
- **There's More Space Around Your Home** - This is going to be the benefit that you're going to be able to visually observe the most. The fact that your house suddenly seems a lot more spacious when it doesn't have unnecessary piles of stuff cluttering every available corner. You will feel lighter, more relaxed, and even a sense of satisfaction and having freed up all this extra space around you. You begin to feel that you have more room in your life for the things that matter.

Defining Your Purpose

As with anything else that we pursue in life, we all need to have a purpose. A reason *why* we're doing what we do. What motivates us, what pushes us to want to succeed, we all need a purpose that drives us to become better.

People choose to embark on a minimalist journey for a variety of reasons. It is a very personal experience, and it could mean different things to different people. Some people do it for the betterment of their mental or physical health, others do it to create more harmony in their surroundings and fluidity in their life, some do it because they're tired of living with so much clutter in their home, and then there are those who choose to do it because they want to reduce their carbon footprint on earth by going with the minimalist approach. Your reason does not have to be the same as theirs, you could do it for your own personal reasons. It doesn't matter what that reason is, as long as *you can clearly define it*, because this reason is going to be the driving force and the motivator that is going to help you stick to this new regiment in your life.

The initial stages of this process are going to be the hardest for some (maybe even all) of you who are reading this book right now. The very idea of tossing out or donating most of your possessions and clearing the clutter is going to make some of you want to turn around and run in the other direction. This is why defining your purpose, finding a strong enough reason to motivate you, is so important. It is going to help you get over the hurdle at the start of this process that is going to challenge you the most. But, like everything else, once you've started, it's eventually going to get easier as you go along and start reaping the benefits and the rewards that await you.

Who Is Minimalism For?

The answer is, *everyone*. That's the beauty of this concept. Minimalism is an approach that everybody can practice because it does not force you to add here to any strict set of rules. It is completely personal and motivated by your own goals. This is not a concept that is going to force you to be miserable, having to get rid of some of your favorite things in life. It's not going to force you to toss out your favorite pair of jeans or ask you to get rid of your car or downsize your home (unless you want to). There is nothing *forced* about practicing this way of living at all. It is about doing what is best *for you,* and to teach you it is possible to be happy with fewer things instead of more.

One of the biggest challenges you are going to face is having to change your mindset, but we'll talk about that in another chapter later on. Yet another problem with this materialistic world that we live in is that we are constantly surrounded by advertisements and commercials. All subliminally telling us that we *must have* or *need* something. It's on the radio, on television, and absolutely on social media. It is inescapable. Every day, all we need to do is log onto any one of our social media accounts and within the first 5 minutes, you'll have definitely seen more than 2 ads at the very least as you scroll through your newsfeed. Heck, we're even surrounded by ads when watching a video on YouTube or simply checking our emails. This constant exposure is working on our psyche without us even realizing it, which is the reason we end up with a lot of unnecessary items in our life which are not necessities or essentials for survival. That's because these commercials are portraying the notion that we *need* these items in our lives to be happy or feel fulfilled. But do you *really?* Think about the last time you bought something because you thought it might make you feel happier. Did it? How long did that happiness last?

Retail therapy is another trap word which leads us to believe that spending money and making purchases we don't need equates to happiness. Again, this type of happiness is short-lived, and it will never last no matter how much you think it will. Sure, it can alleviate your stress and make you feel a burst of happiness for a short span of time, but once that happiness fades, you're left with something you're most likely never going to use, less money in your bank account which you could have saved, and more clutter around your home — all while still being unable to fill that empty void within you. Why? Because you are relying on external factors to provide you with the kind of happiness that you seek, instead of seeking it from within.

But that is about to change *right now*.

10 Reasons Why A Minimalist Lifestyle Is Going to Be Good for You

When you think about minimalism, what is the first image that pops into your mind? Is it just an empty room with plain white walls, maybe just two or three pieces of furniture? Well, only if you want it to be. Minimalism is about finding an approach that suits you and your lifestyle the best, something which you can be happy with. No one person is going to have the exact same experience or the same way of living when it.

If you need a little more convincing that a minimalist lifestyle is going to change your life for the better, here are 10 reasons that highlight just how beneficial this approach can be:

- **Reason 1: Do You Want to Be More Productive?** Believe it or not, your material possessions, everything that you own and have in your home right now, is taking up a lot more of your time than you realize. How much time do you spend clearing up your home? How much time do you spend on your tech devices aimlessly browsing through social media or other distracting websites? How much time do you spend arranging and rearranging stuff around your home or your office workspace whenever you feel things are getting too messy? The more you own, the more time you end up wasting on doing unnecessary cleaning and clearing. Valuable time which could instead be spent on working towards achieving your goals, or doing something to better yourself. All the material possessions demand a lot more of our time to upkeep then we realize. Do you want to make the most of your time more productively? Go minimalist.

- **Reason 2: You Hate Cleaning.** Some people love it; others detest it. If you're in the latter category, then you're going to love this minimalist lifestyle because less stuff means less cleaning! Since minimalism is only about keeping what you really need in your life, you're going to realize just how much simpler life is when you have fewer things to clean around your home. This is by far absolutely the simplest way to cut down your cleaning time.
- **Reason 3: You Want to Increase Your Savings.** Buying less material possessions means more money for you to put aside into building your savings nest egg. Especially if you've gotten into the habit of making purchases with your credit card. It's time to stop accumulating debt and stuff around the home by simply *buying less and saving more*. Minimalism is going to encourage you to spend money on fewer things, and how to instead spend money on *quality things* that are going to last you much longer. In the long run, this will save you a lot more money down the road.
- **Reason 4: You Want to Be Stress-Free.** We don't realize just how much stress the things in our life can cause us, and how distracting they can be too. When one of your tech devices breaks down around the home, you get stressed. When your clothing items get ruined, you get stressed. When you come home after a long day at work only to find a mess waiting for you at home, you get stressed. We don't realize just how much our external physical environment can contribute to the way that we feel until we really think about it. When you reduce the amount of clutter in your life, the distractions and the stress that you feel is going to be significantly reduced, which in turn will help you feel more relaxed and lead to a more stress-free life.
- **Reason 5: You Want to Do Something Good for the Environment.** From individuals to big corporations, it seems that everyone is concerned with going green these days to preserve our precious environment for the future. You too can do your part for the environment by choosing to live a minimalist lifestyle because by relying on fewer resources, you are thereby reducing your carbon footprint impact and the amount of waste that you produce in the environment. Being environmentally conscious has been the reason that some people choose to become

a minimalist, and if this reason is good enough to fuel you, then, by all means, go for it.
- **Reason 6: You Want A Change in Your Life.** Do you feel it's time for a big change in your life? We all reach a point sometimes where we're tired of the routine that we have now because it no longer brings us any joy or contentment. Many people actually desire for change; they just don't know what to do sometimes. If you've had this same desire but felt at a loss about what to do, why not try something simple like adopting a minimalist way of living to start? It is a gradual change that you can introduce into your life in stages, which makes it a great option for those who *want* to change things up, but don't want to do anything too drastic which they might regret later on. Think of this approach as spring cleaning your home to start with.
- **Reason 7: You've Realized You've Become Far Too Materialistic.** Sometimes, it just hits you like a bolt of lightning. The realization that your life is not where you want it to be, or hoped it would be. When that realization hits is when you know that something needs to be done to make a change for the better. If it has dawned on you that you may have become far too caught up in the materialistic lifestyle that you have lost touch with everything that once mattered to you, this could be a time when you start to adopt a minimalist approach to living.
- **Reason 8: You Want to Improve Your Relationships**. Having so much going on in your life can cause you to neglect the relationships that you have in your life. You're not doing it on purpose, but it just happens without you even realizing it. By reducing the amount of clutter, you've got going on in your life in every aspect (not just your home environment), taking away those distractions will help you reconnect and focus once more on the people who matter in your life and what's important. The less time you spend on the materialistic aspects of your life, the more time you have to spend on the ones who truly enrich your life and give it meaning.
- **Reason 9: You Want to Find Your Purpose Again.** Feeling like you have lost your way in life is not a fun emotion to experience. Nobody wants to feel that way if they could, because it makes you start to wonder and question what you've done with your life so far. When not dealt with productively, this can lead to a lot of negative thoughts which could cause you to spiral into unhappiness, maybe even depression on more serious levels. Living life as a minimalist is going to teach you how to appreciate the things in your life that you value most. To look beyond just making the next purchase that you think is going to make you

happy and instead, focus on being happy with what you already have.
- **Reason 10: You Want A Much Simpler Life.** It can be exhausting trying to live a life where you are constantly trying to Keep Up with the Joneses. Trying to always compare yourself with the people you know, or always trying to one-up them to show that you are living a better life, or you can afford more. It is mentally draining to stay on that kind of path for a long time, and if you're ready for a life that is so much simpler but a lot more meaningful, then it's time to start living life the minimal way and witness just how much your life is going to change for the better when you're not always pursuing the wrong things.

CHAPTER 2
What's Life Like As A Minimalist Anyway?

Remember that image of what minimalism is that was pointed out in Chapter 1? The stark white walls, minimal pieces of furniture around the home? That is an example of what a minimalist myth is. Living a minimalist lifestyle doesn't mean you need to toss out almost all your belongings and live with barely anything like a hermit. It is mainly about re-evaluating what your priorities are so you can eliminate all the things that don't matter in your life. This includes the material possessions around your home, bad habits, behaviors, relationships, even beliefs that don't serve you any good. If something doesn't add any benefit, or even value into your life and who you are as a person at this moment, then you could probably live life without it. *That's* what being a minimalist is.

Why the minimalist lifestyle approach is now being adopted and embraced more is because many people are starting to realize that there is a limit to the happiness that these materialistic possessions can bring. For example, buying a car which costs $20,000 might make you very happy, but buying a car that is $100,000 isn't necessarily going to make you five times happier what you were when you bought the $20,000 car. A watch which costs $30 is going to work the same as a watch that costs $300. They both tell time and that's what they're there for.

Having fewer possessions does not mean your life is going to be any less satisfying. Less stuff could, in fact, make you happier than you ever were before because you learn to appreciate what you have. Minimalism teaches us that it is not about the quantity, but rather it is the quality that matters more. That it is better to have a few treasured possessions that last a lifetime instead of piling your home and life with numerous items that are not bringing you any significant benefit. In the pursuit of happiness, there are many roads and paths to take, one of these roads to live minimally and focus on only what matters in you.

Busting Through the Myths of Minimalism

Minimalism is essentially an ethos; that is what this concept is at its core. It focuses on filling your life with a sense of purpose, a tool to give you the freedom you have been seeking all along, a way to finally cope with what has been overwhelming you by decluttering your life. It is meant to help you unblock the mental clutter that you may have been struggling with.

As you are preparing to embrace this new way of life, it is time to bust through the inevitable myths and misconceptions that have come to surround what it means to live this lifestyle. The sooner you break through the misconceptions, the easier it will be to transition into this new life. Here's what a minimalist lifestyle *is not* about:

- **Myth #1: It Means You Can Only Own A Set Number of Things** - Minimalism is a very personal, individual experience. No two people are the same, and no one is going to live the same life, with the same number of belongings, or live life with the same set of circumstances. Being a minimalist doesn't mean you can only own a certain number of items to your name because not everyone is going to *have the same* number of items. No rule says you only get to keep 10 t-shirts and that's it. Or that you can only have 5 pairs of shoes in your home. This kind of rule does not work, since some people may require more than 10 shirts or 5 shoes, while others could make do with less. It is about finding what works for you. Whether you have 50 or 100 things, it *does not matter*. If the 100 items are functional, serve a purpose and are bringing your life some benefits, then go ahead and keep it.
- **Myth #2: It Means You Can Only Keep What's Practical and Functional** - A minimalist lifestyle is not meant to strip you of joy. If you own one or two items that bring you joy or happiness, but don't necessarily serve a practical or functional purpose, it is perfectly okay to keep them. Minimalism is about being happy with what you have in your life, and it is meant to teach you that you don't need an *excess of stuff* to be happy. Keep what's practical and functional to help you survive comfortably, but if something brings you happiness, you don't have to toss it away. This lifestyle is meant to bring you joy, not strip you of everything that makes you happy. Adopting this minimalist way of living but being unhappy at every moment is not what this journey is about.
- **Myth #3: It Means You Have to Live in A State of Deprivation** - There a Swedish word that described minimalism, and that word is *lagom*. This word defines minimalism is being "enough, being adequate, being sufficient, and being just right." *Lagom* has also been translated widely as "perfect-simple," "moderation" and "in balance." What you will notice about these descriptors is that none of them connote deprivation. One of the most common myths and misconceptions that surrounds a minimalist lifestyle is that you have to live a life of simplicity, depriving yourself of most material possessions. That is not an entirely accurate picture. It isn't about depriving yourself, but rather making your life more functional by only keeping what's practical and serves a purpose.
- **Myth #4: It Means I Have to Decide What Needs to Go Immediately** - Remember in Chapter 1 that it is going to be a daunting task. The idea of decluttering your life, well, where do you even begin? How do you decide what should be kept and what should be tossed out? Take it easy, slow it down, because deciding

what should stay and what should go is not something you need to do right this minute. Sure, you've decided that you want to live life as a minimalist, but that doesn't mean you should immediately start going around your home tossing out all the things which you could live without. This is a myth because it is perfectly okay to take your time with this process. The clearing and decluttering can be done over the span of a few days, weeks, even months if you need to. It's about what works for you, always remember that.

- **Myth #5: It Means That You Can Only Own Black and White Items** - Don't believe everything that you see in the pictures. Yes, there are black and white images that represent what minimalist homes look like. Yes, they look absolutely beautiful, especially the homes with white, wide open, airy spaces which are filled with natural sunlight. However, those are just a representation. In movies and in pictures, those representations do not spell out what your life needs to be like. You don't need to have only black and white possessions to be able to dub yourself a minimalist. Have any color scheme you want. Have multiple color schemes if you want. It is your life, and the choice is entirely up to you. Those pictures and movies are merely there to serve as inspiration, if you like what you see and it works for you, go ahead and model your life after it. But if it doesn't? No problem. Your home and your life should be a reflection of *who you are*, not strip you entirely of your belongings and your personality. If bright, loud colors that pop is who you are, then bright, loud colors it is.
- **Myth #6: It Means You Should Only Live in a Tiny Home** - The size of your home does not matter, which makes this a complete myth. Of course, if you love smaller homes and you genuinely want to live in one, you should. But if you have a perfectly comfortable home that you think you should move out from just because you're not choosing to be a minimalist, that's not being practical. That's because smaller homes do not necessarily work for anyone. A single person may do well in a smaller home and be perfectly content, but if you have a family with kids, a smaller home might only make things more cramped and make everyone uncomfortable. Again, go back to making it *work for you* (this should be your mantra going into this new life). The size of your home does not determine your life as a minimalist. Big homes, small homes, it doesn't matter. You can still get them decluttered either way.
- **Myth #7: It Means You Can't Spend Money Anymore** - Well, you will be spending less money as a minimalist, but not because you *can't*. It's because you're inevitably making fewer purchases, which is going to lead to spending less money anyway.

Minimalism is going to teach you to be intentional about your spending, not curb your spending entirely. The reason this is a complete myth is that it is *impossible* to live life without spending a dime. There will be moments when you need to spend money, that's unavoidable, but being conscious of your spending is going to be the difference and the change in your life right now. Minimalism is going to change a lot of things in your life, and your mindset about your spending is one of them, which will be discussed in another Chapter later on.

- **Myth #8: Minimalist Don't Have Any Style** - Don't let the downsizing your wardrobe bit fool you. Just because you're only keeping the bare essentials, it doesn't mean that your style has to be sacrificed. Not at all. If all the clothes you already own are style and suited to your personality, there isn't even going to be that much difference in your style, except that you'll only be keeping the clothes that you wear and use often and donating the ones you no longer use for need. Being a minimalist also does not mean that you have to only buy drab and simple clothing. You can continue to buy the clothes that fit in with your personality, except now you're only going to be buying them when there's a genuine need for it. You're not going to be rushing to keep up with the latest trends anymore because there is no real need for it, but that doesn't mean that your style is going to be downsized to boring in any way.

- **Myth #9: Minimalism Is Something That Can Easily Be Defined** - Now, this is a myth is because minimalism is a philosophy. Hence, it is not something that can easily be defined. Sure, you can explain what minimalism is, but *defining it* is a whole other story. It is a concept that does have consistent themes to it, but because this lifestyle is something that is going to be a different experience for everybody, it is, therefore, hard to define it easily. Each person is different, which means that their approach and their ideas to minimalism is doing to differ. The themes may be consistent, but defining them altogether? That's not entirely possible.

- **Myth #10: Minimalism Is Not A Sustainable Lifestyle** - It is only not sustainable if you don't want it to be. That is why one of the consistent themes of a minimalist lifestyle is to *make it work for you*. Because if it doesn't work, then yes, it is not going to be sustainable. You won't be happy, you won't be reaping the benefits of what this concept is meant to offer you, and because you're unhappy, it won't be long before you give in to the temptation to revert back to your old way of life. Minimalism can be a sustainable lifestyle if you make the necessary changes to suit the way that your life is now.

Jumping right into the minimalist lifestyle is not going to be easy, and you shouldn't expect it to be. Like every major change in your life, expect it to be somewhat difficult as you go through the initial adjustment period and get used to the new way of doing things. Don't worry too much about the myths and misconceptions of living life as a minimalist; take it one step at a time and give yourself time to adjust to the process. You'll get there eventually, and remember that there are no forced concepts or rules with minimalist living. Only make changes that you feel comfortable doing because you should never feel deprived or unhappy in any way.

How Minimalism Is Going to Change Your Life

No more fancy, extravagant, over the top purchases that you barely use or don't even really like at the end of the day, cluttering up your home just because you felt the need to buy it at the time. A minimalist keeps it simple. They only keep the essentials which are needed for a comfortable, happy life. Aside from all the money that you are going to save by making fewer purchases, another change that you are going to see in your life is that you will no longer be living above your means.

Yes, there is a way for you to finally get out of living paycheck to paycheck cycle because as a minimalist, you will no longer be caught up with the consumerist way of living. Our wants always seem to surpass what we can afford, which is why turning to minimalism is the way to get out of this never-ending cycle of constantly feeling like you're struggling to keep up no matter how much money you may be earning. The more you earn, the more your wants seem to "suddenly" increase. Minimalism going to teach you to live comfortably with what you have and putting a stop to that desire to always keep up with the latest trends and fads because you no longer feel that desire to seek happiness in materialistic possessions.

The life of a minimalist is going to affect your life in several stages. As you begin to ready yourself for this new lifestyle, you're going to learn the difference between what is essential in your life, and what isn't. You're going to be able to distinguish what's important and what isn't. Where previously you would simply make purchases on the spur of the moment, this time, you're going to give each purchase careful thought and consideration, asking yourself, *do I really need this? How is this going to benefit my life? Is this a necessity or can I survive without it?* This is the part where you begin moving away from the materialistic life that you were once so caught up with. Not only is the change going to affect your physical environment, but you will also notice a shift in your mindset and the way that you think moving forward.

The areas of your life in which minimalism is going to inflict a change include:

- **Your Home** - This one is going to probably be the biggest and most noticeable difference in your life. The clutter is going to diminish, and you're going to observe that your home is going to be filled with significantly less stuff and more space. Every available corner of your home is no longer going to be filled with items that you don't use or don't even remember having. Tackling the decluttering of your home is going to happen in small stages, but once it's done, you're going to step back and see a big difference in your home. Take before and after pictures and compare them side by side to see the change right before your eyes.

- **Financially** - Before minimalism, you might have been making steady income every month, but somehow it never seemed to be quite enough to cover everything that was needed. You might have found it hard to save enough each month, and as you begin to take stock of your life, you'll be shocked at just how much you were spending on a lot of unnecessary purchases. You may not have necessarily been living an extravagant life, but you may not necessarily be living frugally either. Once you begin this new lifestyle, you're going to start keeping track of where and what precisely your money is being spent on, with regular reviews on whether there are unnecessary expenses being tacked on. If there are, and they are non-essentials, then it's time to remove them.
- **The Time You Have on Your Hands** - Clutter isn't just around your home; it's in your life too. Before you adopt a minimalist approach, your calendar may have been full. So full that you found it difficult to have any time for yourself. Social gatherings, business meetings, family commitments, you always seem to be running from one event to the next. Minimalism is going to help you reclaim all that lost time so you can finally *make time* for what's important - *yourself.* As you begin decluttering other aspects of your life, minimalism will teach you (in keeping with the whole theme of the process) to only accept the invitations and commitments that are important. The ones that matter and the ones that bring you happiness. You will learn to decline the invitations that you don't necessarily want to go to. Your time is yours to determine what you want to do with it.
- **Your Health** - Because you would have decluttered your calendar and made more time for yourself, you now have the benefit of redirecting that extra time into doing something good for yourself. Such as taking care of your health. With more time on our hands, you'll be able to invest in time to exercise, and prepare meals at home, which are much healthier than resorting to fast food or take out (which you previously might have done far too much off because you were pressed for time, rushing from one appointment to another). With more time on your hands, you could even start spending the weekend meal-prepping for the week if you're not keen on cooking after a long day of work. Not

only is cooking your own meals at home going to be much better for your health, but it is also much better for your wallet too, another wonderful side-effect of minimalism.
- **The Relationships in Your Life -** The honest truth is, not every relationship in your life is important. Even the relationships that you *think* are important. With minimalism, you're going to learn how to invest time and energy into the relationships that truly fill your life with meaning, like the ones with your family, significant other, husband and friends whom you have known for years. In doing so, you will find that you become a much better friend and listener because you're more invested in the relationship.
- **You Learn to Appreciate Your Own Company -** With fewer distractions in your life and more time to focus on yourself, you'll learn to appreciate being in your own company. Minimalism will teach you to reconnect with yourself, to find happiness within yourself again and learning to be happy and content with life as you know it. You'll come to realize that you don't need to be out shopping, spending time with people or spending countless hours browsing your social media newsfeed to find some semblance of happiness. You'll come to realize that you're capable of being perfectly happy sitting at home with a good book and a warm cup of coffee on any given day.
- **You'll Find You're Much Calmer -** Another happy side effect of minimalism is that life will become a lot less stressful when you don't have so much going on in your life. We often think that we need to be busy, that we need to fill out lives at every waking moment in order to feel happy and fulfilled. But nothing could be further from the truth. Decluttering is going to free up not just your life, but your stress levels too because when you've got significantly fewer things to worry about, what is there to stress about?
- **You'll Be More Productive at Work -** That's right, being a minimalist is also going to spill over into your career too. Once you see how beneficial decluttering your home can be, you'll immediately want to declutter your office space too. Removing the distractions from your work environment, even if it is just within your cubicle, is going to make you a lot more productive because you will no longer have distractions pulling your focus away from what you should be focusing on, which is work. You'll be able to get more things done in a day, you'll be able to work through your tasks efficiently, and as a bonus, your boss is going to be very happy with you because of it.
- **Your Priorities Will Change -** Another big shift in your life is going to be the difference you notice in your priorities. As you

begin unpacking your life, removing all the elements that are unnecessary and not actively contributing to your happiness, your priorities are going to change in a good way. The things that you once thought matter will no longer seem so important, while the things that you have forgotten or might have previously taken for granted are what you reconnect with again. Everything about your life is going to change once you start living life as a minimalist, but don't worry because this change is going to be for the better.

CHAPTER 3
Where It All Begins

You're almost ready to begin your new minimalist lifestyle, and in this chapter, you're going to be covering the basics about getting started on this new transformative way of life. To recap, what we have come to understand so far is that minimalism is not a one-size-fits-all solution since each person is going to be undergoing their own unique experience. There is no one way to approach this concept and thus, you have to work around finding solutions that are going to be suitable for you.

If we take a good, long look at the world around us, there are actually plenty of prominent individuals who are already practicing minimalism in some form that we can draw inspiration from. Facebook founder Mark Zuckerberg is one such example, adopting a minimalist approach when it comes to his clothing options. Zuckerberg is always seen donning a simple t-shirt and jeans, and even his t-shirts are often the same color scheme. The late Steve Jobs was another prominent figure who adopted a minimalist approach to his clothing choices, opting for basic black t-shirts and a simple pair of jeans. Efficient, and cost-effective. Other celebrities or successful individuals who have chosen a minimalist approach to living include Warren Buffett, who, despite his wealth, has been living in the same home that he purchased way back in 1958. Keanu Reeves is another celebrity who has opted out of a lavish lifestyle for a much more simple, minimal approach, choosing instead to live in a modest home and often takes public transport just like any other average citizen.

Making the Transition into Minimalism

Now, this is going to be where the most challenging part of the whole process begins. The transition out of your old lifestyle into your new one is where a lot of people struggle the most. As with everything else, it's going to take time to make the necessary adjustments, so don't be too hard on yourself if you find that you're struggling in the beginning. You're about to change almost everything in your life as you know it, a transition period is to be expected. Nobody can turn their lives around completely without facing difficulty at some point along the way.

To keep yourself from feeling discouraged as you begin this big life transition, the following exercises will be good advice to keep in mind:

- **Baby Steps** - Avoid the urge and temptation to immediately jump right in there and start clearing and decluttering your entire life and home all at once. This is a major project, especially when it comes to your home, and you cannot expect it all to be done in one day. It just simply is not possible. Instead, expect the process to span over a few weeks (depending on the size of your home especially), and remember that there is no reason to rush. The more you try to rush the process, the more discouraged you may find yourself when at the end you're completely exhausted, tired, and start to wonder why on earth you decided to begin this monumental task in the first place. This is going to be like climbing a hill, pace yourself and take baby steps. You're not in a race with anyone.

- **One Area at A Time** - When it comes to your home, instead of trying to clear everything all at once, aim to tackle one area at a time instead. Do it in stages or sections, depending on how busy your schedule is and work your way from there. Again, you're not in a race with anybody, so it's perfectly okay to take your time working through this process. Aiming to clear off small sections bit by bit will make the entire process seem a lot more manageable and doable. Some items may require some thought before you decide whether to part with them or keep them and if you rush yourself through the process, you could end up tossing something that you might regret later on. Eventually, before you know it, you would have cleared off your entire home and completed the home environment phase of your minimalist journey.

- **Make a Daily List** - Given that decluttering is an ongoing process, what will help you along the way is to have a daily list that you could work on. Making a list is great for this process because it will help you stay organized and it is much easier to keep track of what's been done and what hasn't. Each day, write down the decluttering goals that you hope to accomplish by the end of the day and it will give you something to focus on. For example, if what's on your list today is to clear out your bookshelf, then focus on that and see how much you can accomplish by the end of the day. Having a visual list that you can look at helps you feel more productive during this process too. Humans are very visual creatures, and we often need to see something right there in front of us before our minds can catch up and start believing in it. When you see a list in front of you that reminds you of what needs to get done, it automatically fuels your motivation because it's reminding you of a goal to work on. If you don't manage to finish a task that is on your list, not a problem, push it to the next day. There is no need to put any added pressure on yourself, baby steps. Remember, baby steps.

- **Having Your Own Rules to Follow** - Wait, what? I thought there were no hard and fast rules in minimalism? There aren't, but there are *personal rules* which you can enforce for yourself when you start to transition into this lifestyle. These rules should only be for yourself and your benefit because you are the one who is living this life now (unless you've got your family involved). The set of rules you can start enforcing for yourself should be both simple and practical. One example of a rule could be that each time you make a purchase other than the essentials like food, groceries and other monthly supplies, you should remove one item from your home. If you were purchasing a new rug, for example, it should be to replace an old rug which you are going to remove from your home as soon as you've made the new purchase (to avoid clutter). Minimalism is not going to stop you from making any new purchases but is going to help prevent you from accumulating clutter around your home. Another example of a rule that you could set for yourself is to only replace an item in your home if it genuinely needs replacing.

- **Start On a "Free" Day** - Beginning the transition into minimalism is best done on a day when you have no prior obligations and commitments going on. This will leave you with the necessary time to really focus on the process when you're not thinking about other tasks that you need to take care of. Once you have decided that you would like to embrace this new lifestyle, look at your calendar and consider which day would be best for you to commit to getting started with the process. Beginning on a weekend would be a good place to start since you most likely do not have to worry about any prior work commitments or arrangements on that day. You want to commit your time to only focusing on making the transition on this "free" day because it's going to take a lot more out of you than you initially realize. Take a day where you can process everything that is happening, and focus on what needs to get done for the day without having to worry about your next business meeting or errand that needs to get done.

Bad Habits You Need to Start Getting Rid Of

Transitioning into minimalism is not just going to be about decluttering and changing up your environment; it's about making changes in other aspects of your life too. As you leave a lot of things behind moving forward, one of these is going to be bad habits that you should start getting rid of to make your new life as a minimalist easier.

- **Give Up Filling Up Your Wardrobe** - If a priority for you is to save yourself a lot of time each morning getting ready and dressed for the day, then one of your goals would be to work on decluttering your wardrobe first. Downsizing it and keeping it simple will save you *a lot* of time getting dressed in the morning because when you only have a few options on hand, the decision-making process is much quicker. Jobs and Zuckerberg chose a minimal wardrobe for a reason. They did not care that people might see them as wearing the same outfit over and over again. They cared about being practical and functional because they knew there were bigger goals to focus on. When it comes to downsizing your wardrobe, make it easier on yourself by focusing on keeping only the pieces which are considered essential staples and clothing items that make you look and feel good when you wear them. Items which you may not have worn or touched in years can be donated, and items which are too worn out to be donated can be tossed or repurpose if you know what to do with them. By making a commitment to simplifying your wardrobe, you're going to find you're a lot more efficient not just in getting dressed in the morning, but in your shopping habits too, which will slowly adjust to fit your new habits and priorities.

- **The No Duplicates Rule** - Have you previously been guilty of perhaps buying the same item more than once? Or maybe purchased an item only to find that you already had the same item in your home, you just forgot about it. One example would be the same blouse or shirt, but in several different colors which you purchased at the time because you thought they looked good. It turns out, you only use perhaps one or two of those items and the rest lay forgotten in your closet. As you start to transition into minimalism, start enforcing the no duplicates rule when you're decluttering and the next time you're about to make a purchase. Ask yourself why do you need several pieces of the same item? Are they going to serve a functional and practical purpose? Minimalism is all about keeping things simple, practical, beneficial and efficient. Now, with this no duplicates rule, it would depend on the context. You don't need multiple copies of the same book for instance, but if you were to adopt Jobs or Zuckerberg's approach to clothing, then you might have to have duplicates of the same t-shirt and jeans to last you the week (see what is meant by there is no hard and fast rule in minimalism?).
- **Avoid Making Comparisons** - Minimalism is going to teach you how to stop comparing yourself to others, and this is something you should start working on as you begin the transition into this process. Comparison will only serve to leave you dissatisfied and unhappy because no matter what it is never going to be enough. Someone is always going to have something better, or own something grander, or dress better. It's a never-ending cycle. You're going to constantly feel inadequate if you're always looking over at someone else's greener grass. So don't. It is time to stop the comparison and start focusing on your own life. Embrace and be grateful for everything that you have in your life right now and free yourself once and for all from the burden of constant comparison.

- **Give Up Procrastination** - We all know it is a bad habit, yet many of us still end up doing it. Procrastinating and delaying things, putting it off to the last minute and when the time comes to finally do it, you feel rushed and stressed because everything seems to be piling on all at once. If you really think about it, there is no real reason to procrastinate something, is there? Things still eventually have to get done anyway, all you're doing is postponing the inevitable and in doing so, you're creating a bigger workload for yourself because there will be other tasks which need attending to. Maybe you've thought of spring cleaning your home for a long time to get rid of some of the mess that has been piling up, but you've been putting off for some time now because clearing your home is a lot of work. However, before you know it, you're looking around at the clutter that seems to have tripled in size and you're wondering *how did it come to this?* That's what procrastination can do, and that's why it is a bad habit that needs to be dropped as you make room for bigger and better changes. If you've been putting off clearing and decluttering your home and your life, then now is as good a time as any to drop that bad habit once and for all as you begin to prepare for the minimalist way of living.
- **Giving Up the Addiction to Social Media** - Ah yes, another one that many are going to struggle with is to learn to let go of the social media addiction that has you spending countless, aimless hours on your phone. While it is okay to check up on your social media accounts maybe once or twice in a day, spending far too much time on social media than you should is when it starts becoming a problem. Social media does not serve any functional purpose, other than to take away your focus from other, more important tasks, expose yourself to more advertisements encouraging you to make purchases, and comparing your life to the lives of others that you see coming up on your social media feed. All the habits that you want to avoid as you start to embrace minimalism because it isn't going to be about the materialistic lifestyle anymore. It isn't going to be about comparing yourself to others anymore, and as for the ads that you see, you're going to have to block out their subliminal messages encouraging you to make unnecessary purchases that you don't need. In your new minimalist lifestyle, it is time to set some boundaries for the amount of time that you spend on social media.
- **Give Up Always Having to Say Yes** - Giving up this bad habit is going to help you free up a lot more time on your calendar. Believe it or not, you may think you're doing something good by saying yes all the time to the people around you because you don't want to hurt your feelings, but if by saying yes you're *hurting*

yourself, that's not something that is going to be sustainable long term. Especially as you prepare to become a minimalist. As you learn to downsize and only maintain the things that are important in your life, you're going to have to get used to sometimes having to say no, especially when you're biting off more than you can chew. Filling up your calendar to a point where you have no time for yourself now has to become a thing of the past as you start to work on minimizing and downsizing the non-material aspects of your life.

- **Give Up the Excuses** - This is going to be an especially useful habit to dump as you begin clearing away the clutter in your home and work space. There will always be a reason not to throw something away. There will always be a reason why you should say yes to a social event — a reason why you should maintain a certain relationship in your life. The excuses will always be there *as long as you want them to be.* In holding onto these excuses, you're only making the transition into minimalism much harder for yourself, so it is time to ditch the excuses and start thinking practically about what is best for you and your life from this point forward. It is time to put yourself and your happiness first because after all, the whole reason you are making this entire lifestyle change (which is a huge upheaval from what you are used to) is that you want your life to change for the better. Holding onto excuses only means that somewhere down the road when things get too challenging, you'll find plenty of excuses why you shouldn't continue living as a minimalist unless *you break this habit right now*. By getting rid of excuses *to hold onto your excuses,* you're putting yourself one step forward towards being successful at this new lifestyle.

Practicing Mindfulness Meditation

A lot of change is going to be taking place in your life over the next several weeks the minute you decide to embark on a new life as a minimalist. It will be a time of self-reflection, to take a look at what gives your life a deeper meaning, and assessing the things in your life which hold value. Living life as a minimalist is going to give you plenty of time to reflect on everything that has happened in your life so far which has led you to this point, and given all the change that's taking place, it is a good time to spend a few quiet moments meditating on everything that's been going on so far.

Meditation and self-reflection are actually interlinked more so than we realize. These two concepts have certain aspects which intertwine with each other, but the end result is the same, which is to help you reconnect with yourself once more. It gives you a chance to reflect on your life and what is it that you value most, which also links back to minimalism's principles of teaching you to find happiness and joy in the simple things in life. If you're wondering how meditation is going to help you with transitioning into your new lifestyle, the answer is it is going to help you develop an awareness of not just yourself, but with the world around you too. Meditation, when practiced long-term, helps bring a sense of inner peace and balance, enhancing your mental clarity which will, in turn, enable you to sharpen your focus and block out all the distractions that are taking you away from what truly matters.

Meditation and self-reflection are two important tools which are going to help you during this transition period, and you should be taking advantage of it because of the following reasons:

- Meditation helps to improve the relationship with yourself, as well as with other people in your life. We're often surrounded with far too much negativity in our lives, bombarded with images from social media about ideals of perfection that are often unrealistic and only serves to make us question and doubt ourselves. We turn to materialism because we think it is going to bring us a sense of fulfilment, believing what we see in advertisements and on social media. But by turning to meditation to reflect on your life, not only will you rebuild that lost connection with yourself, the outward relationships you have in your life will start to improve too as you become more mindful.
- Meditation and self-reflection teach you how to live in the present, which is also what minimalism endeavors to do. Meditation teaches you how to slow your thoughts and connect with your surroundings, to consistently learn to check in with yourself and how you are doing.
- Feeling overwhelmed is a by-product of a stressful life. Sometimes we feel stuck, unable to move forward because our thoughts somehow cannot seem to connect the way that we want them to. Meditation is a way to help you clear away the mental blocks which may have been preventing you from getting the most out of life so far. Meditation is a process which teaches and trains you how to empty your mind and clear your thoughts, which is exactly what you need.
- Meditation helps to make you more attuned to your emotions, which can help with your feelings of self-worth and happiness when you are reflecting upon your life. It helps you to view the world with a renewed perspective, concentrating less on the negative aspects. Exactly the right frame of mind that you need to get into as you begin the transition into your new minimalist lifestyle.
- Meditation can help to increase your self-discipline, which is a tool that you will definitely need, especially at the start of the minimalism process, to help you navigate those challenging

moments. Mindful meditation is an exercise which requires you to sit alone in a quiet space, uninterrupted for an extended period and once you learn how to block out the noise and focus on your thoughts. That act of having to train yourself to sit in quiet contemplation is where you begin to work on increasing your self-discipline too as you resist the urge to give into the noisy chatter that is threatening to break your concentration.

The first 21 days of any new habit or change that you go through is going to be the most difficult stage. If you can make it through this though, through the initial uphill part, then the rest of the way is going to be as easy as running downhill from that point on. Things will only get easier as you move forward, and during this transitional stage, that is something you need to constantly remind yourself of. Get through the hard parts because it isn't going to last for long, and the effort is going to be well worth it in the end. Before you know it, this new way of living is going to be as easy for you as brushing your teeth in the mornings.

CHAPTER 4
The Rulebook To Living With Less

The rules of minimalism may be arbitrary, but there are certain do's and don'ts that minimalists have in common to help them sustain and be successful in this lifestyle, which is what you are going to explore in this chapter.

No one can deny that material goods have consumed us all. All you need to do is look around at the possessions you currently own. The latest gadgets, cars, new pieces of furniture that you maybe didn't really need, new clothes you haven't even gotten around to wearing yet. No surprise, especially since we're constantly surrounded by advertisements from the moment we wake up. On our mobiles, on the radio, on television, YouTube, browsing the internet, even walking into the local grocery stores and supermarkets you'll see ads plastered everywhere encouraging you to buy, buy, buy.

The mindset that purchases and materialistic goods will bring you the happiness that you seek is exactly the kind of mindset that minimalism aims to bring you out of. The moment you shift out of this way of thinking, you will find that life becomes more meaningful because you're now shifting your focus to on the things that matter. Minimalism is the movement that is needed to counter the rise in consumerism before we lose track entirely of what life should be about. Relationships, health, happiness, friendships, family, those are the real things in life that matter.

It is going to be difficult to part with a lot of your material possessions. Some people, in fact, are going to find this stage extremely difficult when it comes to which of their possessions they are about to get rid of. It is going to be uncomfortable and for some, it is even going to be a sad process. Change rarely ever comes easy, and you are going to have to prepare yourself both mentally and emotionally for this stage of the process.

What *Not* to Do as A Minimalist

Minimalism may not have any hard and fast rules, but there are certain things that those who live their lives this way do and don't do. First, let's take a look at what people who live their lives as a minimalist *don't* do:

- **They Don't Hold onto the Past** - Because minimalists are willing to make the necessary changes which are needed if it means it is going to improve their lives for the better. Not everyone has the willpower and discipline to remove almost everything that they own in favor of a new way of living, *and* resist the temptation to give into making new purchases. Cutting things out of your life can be difficult, and minimalists, and you must be ready to let go of the past before you can move forward for a fresh start.

- **They Don't Force Others to Follow Their Path** - Because the choice to live a minimalist lifestyle is a decision that you have made *for yourself*. You did not *have* to make this choice; you *chose* to do so instead. As a minimalist, you can tell others about your new philosophy and approach to life, but don't expect them to conform and to be like you. It is up to them to live their lives the way that they want, even if you may not necessarily agree with it. Avoid forcing your ideals and your notions about what you think they should or shouldn't do because that's how you will end up alienating the people in your life.
- **They Don't Give into Temptation** - Because it took a lot of effort for them to get to this point, even though they may make it look easy. Every minimalist out there right now started off where you are today, having to make peace with the knowledge that they will now have to resist all their old temptations and be disciplined so that they don't revert back to their old ways and unhealthy habits. Minimalists have trained themselves to be disciplined enough to only buy what they need, and they focus on product quality rather than its aesthetic appeal.
- **They Don't Avoid Their Feelings** - Remember how the initial stages of this process are going to be the most difficult and challenging for many new minimalists? This is why. Some possessions around your home will be items that you've owned for a long time, and though they may not be useful, practical or functional, some of these items will hold a certain sentimental value. A lot of people are attached to their belongings for numerous reasons, and having to part with them is going to be a very emotional process. Those who have mastered the art of minimalist living had to go through that process too, and what they *didn't do* was, they did not try to avoid their feelings. As painful as it may be, you must learn to confront your feelings and deal with it head on, not just in the decluttering process, but in life in general. The suppressing of emotions has never boded well for anyone, and it isn't going to be helpful to you here if you choose to do the same.
- **They Don't Try to Be People Pleasers** - Because you cannot please everyone. It is simply not possible. Even if you think you may have done it, there's one person you're forgetting about - *yourself*. How many times have you found yourself so focused on trying to please everyone that you forgot to ask yourself if you're happy doing what you're doing right now? Too often, most likely. Minimalists understand that there is no necessity to be a people pleaser only to lose yourself in the process, and that is how they

have managed to successfully declutter the non-materialistic aspects of their life by keeping their social circle simple and only focusing on the people and the relationships that matter.

- **They Hold onto the Notion of Being Deprived** - Because they know that you're not "deprived" when you have everything that you need for your survival and to live comfortably enough. If you already have what you need, you will never be deprived. A lot of people are guilty of holding onto a lot of unnecessary items because of the all too common "just in case" or "what if I need it next time" fallacy, which is why they fear being "deprived" if they are without this item. If you haven't used it until this point, you're unlikely to need it anytime soon, which means that it is okay to be without this item and yes, you will survive either way.
- **They Don't Fixate on One Mindset Alone** - Because of your mindset is resistant to change, then the transition to become a minimalist is one that you're going to struggle with immensely. Life is always going to be full of change, some of it good because you find it easy to cope, and some of it bad because you struggle to get through it. Change is inevitable, and if you're fixated on just one type of mindset, expecting everything else to conform according to what you think it should be, minimalism is going to be a very difficult change for you to adapt and accept.
- **They Are Get Confused Between Wants and Needs** - Because minimalists have successfully managed to distinguish between needs and wants. When an urge pops up, they stop to think *do I really need this? Or do I just want it?* Not every urge is going to be a need, and that is something that you too will learn to distinguish over time. It took these minimalists time too to finally be able to separate desires from necessities.
- **The Don't Expect Overnight Miracles** - Because great change always takes time. If you're impatient and hoping to see results almost instantaneously, all you're going to be left with is a lot of disappointment at the end of the day. Minimalists know that this lifestyle is a habit and that it takes work each day to keep that momentum going. They know seeing the results of this change is something which could take anywhere from weeks, perhaps even months before they can see or feel any real difference. Patience, in this case, is really going to be your virtue.
- **They Don't Make Items A Priority** - Because they know that relationships and life experience will always mean more than items ever will. No item will ever be able to fill the lonely void you may experience without meaningful relationships in your life, and no item will ever be able to bring you the kind of lasting, meaningful happiness that you seek. Which is why minimalists embarked on this journey, to begin with because they know that

making items a priority will never be the right path to take and so, they decided to go with an entirely new approach. They don't form personal attachments to their belongings, because they know this will only make it much harder to get rid of.

What You *Should Do* as A Minimalist

This is going to be your new way of living, and you are going to have to make a commitment to stick to this way of living if you want to see a real difference and a change in your life. Whenever we introduce something new into our lives, whether it is a new way of eating, a new routine, or a different way of doing things, it is going to take some time for you to get adjusted before it becomes a habit and a regular part of your life. So again, if it feels tricky and difficult in the beginning, that is okay. Don't be too hard on yourself, and give yourself some time to adjust to this new way of living.

Now that you know what you *shouldn't* be doing as a minimalist, here's what you should be focusing on instead:

- **Make Mindful Purchases** - No more buying on a whim, those days are going to have to be put behind you now. Minimalists still need to shop (they're not completely cut off from the real world, after all), but what they do differently from the rest of us is that they practice *mindful shopping*. This means that they think long and hard about each item before they purchase it, weighing the pros and cons and whether this item is a necessary or essential purpose. They factor in the functionality and practicality of each item, and in what way it is going to enhance their life. It sounds like a lot of work to do before making any purchase, but once you get used to the process, you'll be able to go through the motions without even really thinking about it.
- **They Fix Instead of Buy** - Minimalists no longer immediately toss out an item or piece of clothing if it's broken or torn. They choose to fix their items instead of immediately resorting to making new purchases. Because they focus on buying items which are durable, this process is often successful, saving them a lot of money in the process and valuable time having to shop around for a suitable replacement.
- **They Borrow, Not Buy** - If something can be borrowed, why spend money buying? Especially if you're only going to use the item once or twice and then hardly ever (or never) after that. That's what minimalists do to save themselves time and money again. Borrowing from friends and family will be one of the first options that they would consider, and that is what you need to start thinking about too, once you start living this lifestyle.
- **They Choose High-Quality Items Instead** - Minimalists usually choose to go for the items which are of higher and better

quality, even if they may come with a slightly heftier price tag. That's because minimalists shop with the focus of buying items that are going to last much longer, perhaps even several years. This saves them a lot of time and money compared to if they were to buy the cheaper items, but only to have it break down after several uses. It makes much better financial sense to purchase a one-time more expensive item, but have it last you almost a lifetime. That's just one of the many ways that minimalists help to minimize their expenses.

- **They Look After Their Items** - Since they have so few possessions, looking after each item carefully is not as hard Is that they start to treasure everything that they have as you may think. Minimalists find it easy to care for the possessions that they currently own because each item that they own is treasured, something that they chose to keep when everything else was either tossed out or donated. So looking after them really happens almost instinctively without even having to think much about it.
- **They Are Always Grateful** - A by-product of living with only a few, very treasured possessions is that they come to treasure everything that they have. Becoming a minimalist has put a lot of things puts a lot of things into perspective and cultivating an attitude of gratitude if you will. Minimalism is in part about the search for happiness and contentment, and about helping you realize that those two qualities do not reside within materialistic possessions. This gratitude is exactly what helps them appreciate and be happy with the life that they currently have. When you are content with what you have in your life, it won't be long before that constant urge and desire to have more fades away over time.
- **They Purge Regularly** - With minimalists, decluttering is not just a one-time process. They make it a habit to carry out regular reviews and purges of their belongings, just to make sure that the clutter is not piling up again without them realizing. They could do this every couple of months, maybe even twice in a year, but minimalists purge regularly and comb through the inventory of their belongings. Anything that hasn't been used in a while must go. Anything that does not serve a practical or functional purpose must go. Clothes that you kept during the first round but realized you haven't worn or touched yet must go. They go through their belongings every now and then and eliminate everything that is not necessary. This is how they maintain that minimalistic lifestyle they built in the beginning.
- **They Have Learnt Not to Feel Guilty** - We all own items that we don't necessarily use or want, but we've kept them around because we feel obligated or guilty. These include birthday gifts, random presents from family or friends, souvenirs you may have

picked up on your travels, basically anything in your home that is not essential for your survival. These items continue to remain with us because they could be expensive, sentimental, still in good condition, perhaps even all of the above. Minimalists though have learned to let go of that guilty feeling because they have come to realize that those are *not good reasons* to keep those items around.

Experiencing the Freedom of Living with Less

This experience can be a lot more liberating than you may think. Living as a minimalist, it's not about downsizing all your belongings for the sake of clearing away the mess in your home alone. No, it is much more than that. It is about clearing your entire life and redefining it to have more purpose and meaning than it once did before. You will be amazed at how this experience can bring you a sense of peace.

As a new minimalist, your first goal is to make a commitment to yourself. You need to make a commitment to fully embracing this new change wholeheartedly. Why? Well, simply because you owe it to yourself to live a better life. Having goals throughout this entire process is the key to helping you achieve the most out of living life as a minimalist. This lifestyle philosophy may not have a lot of rules, but there is *one rule* that everyone should abide by, and that is to set up personal goals for yourself as you begin every new journey in your life. Whether it is a new career, a new personal project, a new relationship, anything, setting goals is the key to a successful outcome. Goals help you follow through and remind yourself why you got started in the first place. You know why you chose to begin living as a minimally. You have your reasons, and these reasons must form a concrete foundation, so whenever you start to ask yourself why you began this journey when it gets to the challenging parts, these reasons will be part of your goal setting which will remind you not to give up.

The number one rule of successful goal setting is to have a purpose. Not just any purpose, but a clear purpose and a focal point. Your purpose must be so clear that whenever anyone asks you why you chose to get into this minimalist way of living, you are able to answer without even having to think too much about it. When you have your purpose as clear as day right in front of you, it makes it hard for you to lose sight of the finish line. And that is why you need to define your purpose before you even begin to attend making a list of goals for yourself.

The best way to set clear and defined goals for yourself is to reflect on your current lifestyle. What is it about your current lifestyle that warrants such change? Why do you want to begin a new life as a minimalist? What about your current lifestyle is unsatisfactory right now that is driving you towards this change? Giving your current lifestyle some deep thought and reflection will help you pinpoint exactly what it is you want and hope to improve. It will help you be clear about what you hope to achieve by living as a minimalist. Make it one of your goals to make no excuses. Yes, it may be difficult at some point, but everything in life is not without its challenges. Another goal when you start adopting this minimalist lifestyle is to take it slow and take it small. Don't attempt to be over ambitious right out of the gate, setting overarching goals and then when you fail to meet those goals. You end up feeling disappointed.

Your Minimalist Lifestyle Will Eventually Become a Habit

The general rule is that for something to become a habit, you need to stick to the routine for about 21-days or so. The initial 21-days is when you're going to have to put in most of the hard work into the process and to be disciplined and not give up halfway through when the going gets tough. Stick it out for the first couple of days and minimalism will eventually become a habit that is ingrained and a part of your life. However, you must be consistent. *You must.* Make it a consistent and daily routine, not something that is done a few times a week because that makes it much harder for it to form into a habit. The more effort that you put into making this routine, the easier it will be for it to become a habit. The first 21 days are the most crucial part of the process, and if you don't give it your all during this stage, you're unlikely to achieve the successful outcome that you're hoping for.

What will help make the transition easier is to have positive affirmations. It helps to have little reminders and positive affirmations as to why you started this journey in the first place. It may seem like a pointless exercise and it is easy to brush off "the power of positive thinking" as another ideal that is only preached about but has no real basis, but you'd be surprised at just how effective it can be. Write little positive affirmations on post-it notes and stick them around the places where you are not likely to miss them around your home. Write little motivational phrases to help keep you going and remind yourself not to give up.

Another great strategy that you're going to find useful is to build new habits on a pre-existing habit. Let the old habit will act as an anchor (remember not to choose a bad habit, though). Choose a habit that you don't plan to get rid of. For example, if you already prefer to dress in a simple manner, and already do so on most days, then when you commit to this new minimalist lifestyle, build on that by continuing to choose simple, practical and functional items of clothing to keep in your wardrobe as you work on eliminating the rest.

How Do I Know I'm Doing This Right?

Each day, track how well you did with adjusting and keeping up with the changes and meeting the goals that you set out for yourself. When you keep track of your progress each day, it makes it easier for you to track which areas may be in need of some improvement. Writing down your progress makes it easier for you to see just how far you've come, and therefore, you are more likely to follow through than if you were to just go through each day going with the flow. Tracking your progress a good exercise which keeps you responsible and accountable for how well you are doing, and when you have a strong desire to succeed, it becomes much easier for you to stick to that commitment then you have something that reminds you of just how well you are doing.

Either way, you are doing great just by choosing to start in the first place. Be kind and don't be too hard on yourself, and take everything as it comes one day at a time. You don't need to try and do too much too soon, pace yourself, work through things one and a time and you will eventually get there.

CHAPTER 5
Can I Minimize Other Areas Too?

The answer is, absolutely! Minimalism is not just about decluttering your home environment or your workspace at the office. *Every* aspect of your life can benefit from the concepts and principles of what it means to live life as a minimalist. Keeping it simple and down to only what you need to comfortably survive is something that can translate to a lot of other areas in your life, including your finances, technology, health and the way that you shop or make purchases from now on.

Minimalism and Your Finances

Quite possibly one of the most exciting benefits to look forward to in your new life as a minimalist is how much money you're now going to save when you're not constantly splurging and spending unnecessarily. This is exactly the kind of lifestyle that you would need, in fact, if you were longing to get out of the cycle where you live from one paycheck to the next. Living a life where you're constantly counting the days until your next income boost, only to have the amount flit away before you're even halfway through the month is no way to live. It is stressful, mentally exhausting having to live with that kind of worry, and it is a cycle that is never going to end. Unless you do something about it, that is.

Observe other minimalists around you (if you know of any) and you will notice that one thing they have in common is that they don't live above their means. They don't own the latest of everything, and they don't try to keep up with what the current trends are when everyone else around them is succumbing to the temptation. That's because these minimalists realized something long ago, and that is our wants will always surpass what we can afford. Think about it. As your paycheck gets bigger, do you end up saving more? Or do you find that for some inexplicable reason, your "wants" and "needs" suddenly seem to grow right along with your pay rise and you're back to living from paycheck to paycheck, despite the increase. That's because *our wants will always surpass what we can afford* (write this down and stick it somewhere to remind you of it).

Living a minimalist lifestyle is how you get out of this cycle once and for all. No more will you have to constantly feel like you're struggling to keep up with your expenses, no matter how much money you're earning. You're going to learn how to live comfortably with what you have, and practice minimalism long enough, your materialistic desires will soon ebb away.

To begin downsizing your finances, there are several things which you are going to need to go through. First, you need to make a list of all your expenses — every single one down to the last penny. When you're done, take a look at the list and observe which areas or expenditures are deemed "unnecessary" that you could probably start cutting out of your life. Maybe it's that $3 cup of coffee that you're spending on each morning on your way to work. Cut that out, because making coffee at home will save you a lot more money, and it tastes just as good too. Maybe it is your "monthly ritual" of buying one new pair of shoes each month after payday to "treat" yourself. Cut that out, because you've already got what you need. Observe your expenses with a critical eye and start crossing out the ones that you don't need for survival.

The next step is to work on eliminating recurring debts each month. This includes credit cards, student loans, car loans, mortgage payment, cable bills, gym membership (do you even use the gym as regularly as you would like?), and miscellaneous monthly subscriptions to name just a few. Some people may have different debts of course, depending on their lifestyle, but it is now going to be your goal to eliminate those debts one at a time. Start with your most manageable debt, which for example could be your credit card. Pay them all off, and then cut up your credit cards, so you are no longer tempted to keep using them. Then work on the next debt and the next. Gym memberships are another thing which you could probably do without, especially when you could exercise for free at home. If you don't frequent the gym often enough to make it worth the dollars you're spending, then it's a safe bet to say you could probably cut that out of your life and reinvest that money somewhere else. Miscellaneous expenses like cable bills and Netflix subscriptions, for instance, are also examples of items that are not essential for your survival because you could make do without them. In the spirit of now only living with what you need to survive, if something is not considered a necessary expense for your survival each month, eliminate it and put the money that you saved there into your savings account.

This is going to require a lot of sacrifices (maybe even a *huge* sacrifice) for some people to have to cut out the little luxuries in life they have become so accustomed to. It's going to be challenging, and it is okay to find a compromise towards working on this aspect, so you don't feel so completely deprived. Instead of buying a cup of coffee each morning on the way to work, maybe cut it down to once or twice a week to start until you're completely comfortable weaning it out of your life. It is okay to treat yourself occasionally because minimalism is not meant to strip you of joy. It is simply meant to teach you to spend *most* of the time living life in a simple manner instead of making extravagant and unnecessary expenses a part of your everyday routine. If, every now and then, you do feel like treating yourself, by all means, go for it. It is important to reward ourselves once in a while to keep our motivation going too.

One of the perks of living in the digital age that we do today is that there is an app for literally almost everything. In this case, that's good news because it can help to make your budgeting process a lot easier, perhaps even fun depending on the app that you're using. Budgeting apps are useful to help you keep track of your finances and spending habits on the go, with notifications and reminders to help you stay on track. There are several options to choose from, so pick one that you think works best for you and start taking control of your finances right now.

Minimalism and Your Shopping Habits

As you begin your new life as a minimalist, you will no longer be making purchases the same way you once did. Minimalists have a very different, more efficient way of shopping, as you would probably have already guessed by now. They only shop for want they need, and very rarely do they ever shop for what they *want,* if they ever do at all that is (it is entirely up to you). Now that you are adopting this new approach to living, you are going to have to change your spending habits entirely.

In line with reassessing your finances, you are now also going to have to start creating a strict budget for yourself which you are going to live by each week. It is very important to stick to this budget (unless there is some sort of emergency) and avoid deterring from that budget or giving in to your temptations the way that you may have done previously. What you are most likely going to be spending on weekly is your groceries, and if previously grocery shopping was done without a list, then you will understand just how easy it is to be carried away and end up spending more than you initially thought that you would, especially when there is a reduction in prices for certain items. Creating a budget is a very important step in the reinvention of your shopping habits, and you should try to avoid ever going shopping without a list in hand to help keep you on track.

How often did you stop and think before you made a purchase prior to deciding that you now wanted to become a minimalist? Hardly ever? Or never? That's how most of us end up with a lot of unnecessary items, sometimes duplicate items around the house that we end up storing away and forgetting about. Now that you are about to adopt a minimalist approach to living, every purchase must be accompanied by two actions before you open your wallet and hand over your money. *Stop and think.* Even if the purchase is something as small as a candy bar, for example, you need to stop and think about whether this purchase is necessary and if it is deviating from your budget for the week. For the bigger, more expensive items, even more, thought needs to be put into is. Ask yourself why you're making this purchase. Think about how buying this item is going to help you long-term. Consider if this item is a necessity or a luxury? If you can make do without it, then the honest answer is you probably didn't need it, to begin with. If you can begin training yourself to think this way, you will see what a significant difference it makes and how your spending habits are going to be so different from here on out.

Another way in which your purchasing habits are now going to change as a minimalist is that you will no longer only be focusing on "cheap" items, thinking that it's okay to purchase them because they are cheap enough. They may be on the cheaper side, but how long do they last? Once they do wear out or break down, don't you have to spend even *more* money having to replace them with something else? Making frivolous purchases are now going to have to become a thing of the past because minimalists shop with only one agenda in mind - *looking for items of quality*. Durable items which last much, much longer than the cheaper ones do are going to be so much better long-term because, for one thing, you don't have to keep spending money every few weeks or months having to replace them when they break down. Secondly, higher quality, durable items can often be fixed, which is significantly cheaper than having to buy entirely new items. It is now going to be all about quality and durability when it comes to making purchases.

You're also going to have to do your research whenever possible when making non-grocery item purchases. Whenever possible, do as much research as you can before making any major purchase especially, because this will help you determine which stores will give you the best value for money. Doing research will also let you know if there are alternative options to what you want to purchase, for example, whether it might make more sense for you to DIY the items at home, or if perhaps some of your old items could be repurposed. There are solutions for almost anything these days, which a quick Google search online will reveal. Doing your research will minimize the number of impulse purchases that you make too, which is something you want to get rid of as you begin anew as a minimalist.

Minimalism is going to teach you many things, among them learning the difference between items which are essential, and items which are not. As you learn how to slowly move away from the materialistic lifestyle you were once so consumed with, making purchases will get easier over time and it won't seem so hard to forgo the temptations that once use to persuade you into making purchases that you did not need.

Minimalism and Your Health

Downsizing your life is going to remove a lot of things, one of them is the stress that previously seemed to follow you everywhere you went. A big part of why this consumerist lifestyle was so bad for us is because of all the unhealthy habits and obsessions which it led us to cultivate. Downsizing your life is going to free up a lot of the burden that once weighed you down and took up so much of your time that you ended up having *no time* to focus on what mattered most, which is your health. The consistent pattern that emerges with minimalist living is the theme of keeping things simple and easy to manage, something which could translate into your fitness and nutrition too.

When you start to declutter the unnecessary events and social appointments that you did not necessarily want to attend in the first place, you will have a lot more time to start getting into a healthy workout routine again. You don't need expensive gym memberships either, because you could easily work out in the comfort of your own home, or simply go for a jog in the park, which is free. If jogging is not your style, there are plenty of other workout options which you could find to suit you. At home DVDs or apps that you can download to your phone and follow along too have made it easier than ever for us to take care of our fitness and get in the recommended exercise that is needed to stay healthy. Workouts these days are even tailored to suit your busy schedule, with options that allow you to workout anywhere from 5, 10, or 15 minutes if you're pressed for time.

When you start to create a lot more free time for yourself because you're not constantly rushing from one appointment or errand to the next, you now have the option of preparing more nutritious food at home instead of having to rely on takeout all the time. With your new budget and grocery list in hand, you can take control and make mindful purchases of the food items that you consume. Cooking and preparing your meals at home will always be the choice that makes the most sense, and the choice that is best for your body because you know exactly what is going into your food.

Minimalists are happy with the simple life that they lead because they are not stuck in the *I don't have enough time* mentality. Everyone has the same 24-hours in a day, and minimalists have discovered a way to maximize their time and make it more efficient by cutting out all the unnecessary clutter that they did not need. In doing so, they freed up time for themselves to focus on what matters the most, one of which being their health and nutrition. By eating right and working out several times a week, you will notice quickly how much better your body and your mind feels, and you will be glad you embarked on this journey to change your life for the better.

With the money that you are now saving by eliminating gym memberships and takeaway food, you will now have a little extra wiggle room in your finances to redirect it where it matters, such as towards better healthcare insurance for one thing. Health insurance is essential, especially given the rising medical costs each year. The company that you work for may offer some sort of medical coverage or health insurance, but you should still get your own coverage just in case because you may leave your job anytime in the future to pursue other interests or better career options.

Minimalism and Technology

Technology can be both a good and bad thing, depending on who is using them. Technology can be a beautiful thing because it allows us to stay connected to the people who matter most, no matter where in the world they may be. Family members, friends or lovers who may be on the other side of the world are now a quick phone call or social media app message away. We can easily reach out to the people in our lives on the go, no matter where we may be as long as we have an internet connection on our hands. Or, technology could be a bad thing because it is the cause of us spending countless hours lost in a sea of Facebook posts, Instagram stories and Tweets about the latest happenings. One minute you're checking your phone and the next 3 hours have gone by without you even realizing it.

Minimalists are still living with technology because this lifestyle doesn't require them to be complete hermits, but it is *how* they use this technology that sets them apart from everyone else. Like with all the other aspects in their lives, minimalists limit their use of technology down to the bare minimum, and that is what you need to start doing too as you begin to prepare yourself for this new life. How do they limit their use of technology when it seems that technology is so crucial for everyday survival?

By only focusing on what's important, that's how. Our phones are constantly beeping or pinging each day with an endless barrage of information. From social media updates to emails and what is happening in the news lately, little do we realize that this constant flood of information is disrupting our ability to focus. Remember how social media can cause us to feel unhappy and discontent because we end up comparing ourselves to who seems like they are doing better? That's not doing you any favors, and that is exactly why minimalists keep their social media checking down to the bare minimum because they don't want to be distracted by things that no longer matter. You can still maintain your social media accounts because it is a means of keeping in touch with the people in your life, but instead of checking it every hour or several times a day, limit it to perhaps two or three times a day. Instead of spending an hour or two merely browsing your social media feeds, downsize it to perhaps just 10 minutes or so to get your daily fix and then move onto more important things that matter.

Another way in which minimalists keep their technology usage down to a minimum is to eliminate the gadgets that they don't need. Some people, for example, have more than one phone and perhaps more than one iPad or tablet too. Do you really need multiples of these items? They also do not carry all their gadgets with them at all times, because it distracts from living in the present. If you're on the go and out of your home, then the only device that you're going to need is your mobile phone to be contactable. All the other gadgets do not need to come with you, so leave them at home and focus only on one device at a time.

Minimalists also set designated hours during a day which are "tech-free" hours, meaning that during these hours, there is strictly no technology usage at all. This approach could be employed when spending time with family and friends, or when spending quality time with yourself, reconnecting, meditating, exercising, or simply doing something good for your own benefit. Having technology around will always be distracting, and minimalists approach this hurdle by putting the phones on silent, or putting them away for the time being so they can be more focused on the task at hand and present when they are in the company of others. Even when you're working at the office, having your phone next to your computer as you click away at the keyboard can be very distracting. Putting your phone on silent is not going to be of much help here, because as soon as the screen lights up, your focus will instantly shift from what you're doing to wondering what notification just popped up on your phone. Minimize your use of technology at work by tucking your phone away in your desk drawer during these designated hours where you need to focus on a task. You'll be a lot more productive that way.

Even your computer can be used minimally with more efficiency, and it begins with using your computer with intention. To effectively minimize this area (which seems almost impossible since we spend several hours in a day dependent on our computers for work), you can maximize your time efficiently by eliminating anything on your computer that is not actively contributing to your productivity. When you're able to focus on the task at hand without being distracted, you work through it much quicker, finish faster and thus you minimize the amount of time that you spend on your computer. Who would have thought? Start by first cleaning out your desktop by removing any unnecessary files and folders that you do not use daily or for important work purposes. Save them somewhere else, or delete them entirely if you don't need it anymore. Having a less cluttered, minimalistic view of your desktop will immediately make getting work done a lot more efficient. Uninstall any apps, games and programs that are unnecessary and only serve as a distraction from what your work. Working in full-screen mode is also an effective way to block out distractions, so open up that Word document that you're working on in full-screen mode, so it's nice and big in front of you, making it much easier for you to focus on.

CHAPTER 6
Shifting Your Mindset

In everything that you do, your mindset makes a difference. No matter what situation you may be facing, what challenges you may be going through in life, the minute your mindset shifts is the moment when things will change. How you perceive situations will ultimately shape the reality around you. For life to be better, you need to believe that it *is possible* to change for the better. What we don't realize is that our thoughts have more power over us than we realize, and all you need to do is observe how damaging a negative mindset can be to witness the power of your mind.

A negative mindset will always be an anchor in your life that weighs you down. Minimalism is meant to free you from that old life, but you need to shift your mindset in order for you to get to that point. Yes, minimalism is going to be an upheaval of almost everything in your life, from your belongings, to your social calendar, relationships and now your mindset too.

The first thing we need to change is the way that we think about minimalism. It isn't just about downsizing your possessions and decluttering the mess you have accumulated around your home, and it often gets misunderstood because this is the image that immediately pops into most people's minds as soon as they hear the worlds "minimalism." We now need to shift out of that way of thinking and start to understand that minimalism is more of a state of mind than anything else. Yes, it is about decluttering the material objects from your mind, but it is also about *making room* for the more important things in your life, like your health, relationships, friendships and especially family time.

Most people spend their lives constantly working, working, working trying to earn more just so they can keep up with their wants and buy even more stuff. They think that if they were to earn XXXX amount of money, they would then be happy, only to realize when they are earning the amount that they wanted, they're not truly happy at all. This mindset of thinking that we need "stuff" in our lives to make us happy on top of everything else is exactly the reason why many will spend the rest of their working lives forever trapped in this cycle. It is only with a shift in your mindset, the realization that simplicity can bring you more happiness than stuff ever could is when you begin to experience real change.

Signs That You Need to Start Changing the Way You Think

If you've ever wondered whether your mindset has held you back from accomplishing a lot of things in your life, the answer is it probably has. The fact that you're feeling unfulfilled, that there's more you could have done (or wish you had done), means that your thoughts and perceptions have probably held you back on some level. Which is why it is so important to make a real mindset change *before* you begin your journey to become a minimalist because it is the only way you're going to benefit from all the change that is about to take place.

Let's talk about mindset first in general. Has your mindset been the anchor that held you back all this time? The answer lies in how many of the following situations you find you can relate to:

- **You Mostly Feel Unhappy** - When your mind is stuck on negativity most of the time, or more wired to focus on the bad than the good, you find that you spend most of your waking hours feeling unhappy, miserable and wishing that things could be different. Negativity is a force so strong that it blinds you to all the good things that you have going on in your life, and it makes you forget that you have a lot to be grateful for. This inability to see the silver lining and count your blessings will be the cause of a lot of the unhappiness that you feel. You end up comparing your life to those of the people around you, and the grass will always seem greener on the other side than it actually is. If this sounds a lot like what you're going through now, then you can be sure that it is time for a change.

- **Letting Go Becomes a Struggle** - It is going to be a real struggle for you to declutter the way minimalism requires you to if you find it hard to let things go. Letting go is not an easy process, but when you tend to hold onto to something more than you should, then you're going to find this process a challenge every step of the way. People who find it difficult to let go often struggle attaining emotional freedom, and they hold onto the past more than they should using it as reasons to hold them back from accomplishing future successes. These people might also show a greater tendency to hold onto their belongings for years, unable to part with it because there's always a reason why they should keep it around. Unfortunately, as you make the transition towards a minimalist lifestyle, you're going to have to learn to let go of a lot of things, and that can only be accomplished if you're willing to change your mindset.

- **You're Constantly Making Excuses** - Does this one sound all too familiar? Excuses seem to flow all too easily for just about everything. *I want to be a minimalist, but...... I want to change my mindset, but....* There's always going to be a 'but', a reason why you can't, won't or shouldn't do something. People who allow that to happen are the ones who prefer to make excuses because it is simply easier than making any real effort to change. Whenever someone suggests doing things differently than what you may be used to, you immediately feel put off by it and start

thinking of excuses to get out of doing it. This mindset has got to change if you want to experience all the benefits from this new lifestyle that you are about to immerse yourself into.
- **You Criticise Far Too Often** - Not only do you criticize yourself, but you also do it to the people around you. That's because a negative mindset is wired to look for the flaws and mistakes more so than anything else. Do you do this more often than you should? Do you find yourself being more critical instead of praising yourself or others for their efforts, or commending them on their effort? It is certainly time for that mindset to change if you've found yourself nodding along in agreement as you read this.
- **You Lack Motivation** - Do you lack the desire to do even the smallest and simplest of tasks? Even if it is something as small as perhaps catching up with a friend over a cup of coffee? Lacking motivation is a clear sign of a negative mindset, and if you find that you feel demotivated, tired or drained of energy all the time, this is why. You bail out of plans at the last minute, and you cancel social engagements because "you weren't feeling up to it." This mindset has got to change if you want to *see any real change* happening.

How many of the scenarios above did you find yourself relating to? One? Two? Maybe even all of them? Minimalism is here to teach you to focus on what matters the most in our lives, but that cannot be done if you're holding onto your old thought patterns. The fact that you *want* to change, and *want* a new way of living is a good start, and you need to now use that desire for change to fuel you as you work at overcoming your mindset. You can only truly embrace minimalism and all that it has to offer if you train your mindset to start thinking like a minimalist too.

A shift in mindset is something that is going to happen subtly and happen gradually over time in little ways. You might not even realize that it's taking place until one day it just hits you how much things have changed. How much *you* have changed. Especially when you look around your home and at your life since you decided to adopt this new approach to living, it is only then that you will start to realize just how big of a difference a simple shift in the state of mind can be.

What *Is* A Minimalist Mindset?

People often misunderstand and think that by decluttering the possessions they own; it is the end of life as they once knew it. Don't think of it as an end, but rather a *new beginning*. You have been given the opportunity right now to be "born again," to not waste your life pursuing the wrong kinds of happiness. You are about to awaken to the realization that has been right in front of you all this time, which is that you already have everything you need to be happy. You just forgot about it somewhere along the way. The way you perceive it is going to be the defining difference, and if you choose to see it as the end of an era having to part with your belongings, then that kind of mindset is going to prevent you from seeing everything that you are about to gain.

Clutter surrounds our physical space, and we're often so distracted, consumed or overwhelmed with everything that is happening in our lives each day that we forget there is the other kind of clutter that we also need to deal with — the *mental clutter*. Everyone is living with some form of mental clutter, and it starts to become a problem when it is exacerbated by what is known as mental hoarding. In your physical space, you accumulate and hoard in the form of buying things. In your mental space, you accumulate and hoard when you start to hold onto bad memories, negative thoughts, failures of the past, and present worries that you seem to struggle to forget. This is a very real problem which needs to be addressed, especially since mental health is often overlooked and not talked about enough the way that it should. Compounding all these thoughts in your mind over time with no effective way of dealing with it can take a real toll on the body, and often leads to conditions like anxiety and depression. Yet, many people still feel uncomfortable addressing the very real issued that come with not taking care of your mental health, and minimalists have realized that the only way to renew your mind, to remain calm and focused in the midst of chaos, is to declutter the mind along with everything else.

Here is what it means to live with the mindset of a minimalist:

- You are learning how to choose quality over quantity, and to be grateful for what your life is currently filled with.
- You are learning how to be responsible for your own decisions. Financial decisions, career decisions, social decisions, relationship decisions, any decision that you make you are now going to be accountable for, and you are learning how to *choose* the decisions that will bring about the most value for you.
- You are learning about self-discipline, especially during the hard times when your every impulse is urging you to give in to the desire to buy that item you've been eyeing for so long.
- You are learning to choose what is important to you every day, choices which will ultimately result in long-term happiness.
- You are going to learn how to live in the present instead of constantly worrying about the future as you begin to realize that the present is something that you *do have control* over and worrying about what is yet to happen is not benefiting you in any way.

Removing the mental clutter that is currently blocking your mind is a necessary part of the process because a shift in the mindset cannot happen when your mind is blocking the change from happening. Imagine you were driving down the road and there was a big boulder blocking your path. There is no way to move forward unless you first find a way to remove the obstacle that is blocking your way.

How the Minimalist Mindset Is Going to Change the Way You See the World

As you embrace a life where you live with less and live each day in a simple manner, grateful for what you have, you're going to see the world in a different light altogether. Minimalists call this the *minimalist mindset shift*, and here is how it is going to change the way that you think and view life as you know it:

- **You Begin Valuing Experiences More Than Belongings** - The belongings that once mattered so much to you that you had a hard time parting with will no longer seem so important. As you begin to commit to a life where you learn to live with less, you start placing more value on life experiences instead of worldly possessions. You would, for example, value the time that you spend with your family, husband, children or friends more than ever, because it has become clear that *this* is what fills your life with meaning more than a new purchase ever will. That you would rather "clutter" your mind with wonderful memories instead of the actual stuff. New adventures, travels, experiences, shared stories and treasured memories will become more valuable to you than all the belongings that you own in your life.
- **Shopping No Longer Matters** - For those that used to avidly believe in retail therapy as a cure for what "ailed" them in the past, this is going to be a dramatic shift in the mindset. But this is exactly what is going to happen once you've committed to becoming a minimalist. As you fully embrace and immerse yourself into minimalism, you will become a lot more intentional and mindful about what occupies your space, when you open your eyes and come to the realization that you already have everything that you need to live happily and comfortably, your mindset shifts towards other priorities which do not involve shopping and making new purchases. Joshua Becker's once said that *maybe the life you always wanted is buried under the stuff that you own*, and it couldn't be more apt in describing this situation.
- **You're More Mindful About What Surrounds Your Space** - Once you're done decluttering and minimizing your home and your life, you'll realize that clearing up all that mess was no joke. It took a lot of effort and hard work on your part and the memory of that is exactly what's going to keep you from reverting back to your old habits. Because you don't want to have to go through the entire purging process again, sure, technically you could, but *why would you?* It was hard enough work that first

round, and doing all that again is not going to be a productive use of your time. The remainder of how much work and effort you put into that first round is exactly why your mindset is going to shift to make you more mindful about what you're allowing into your home and your life.

- **Owning Less Becomes a Priority** - As "stuff" takes less precedence in your life, your mindset will gradually change to where owning less now becomes your priority instead. That's because once you fully immerse yourself into the living with less lifestyle, you will see just how beneficial, time-saving and productive it can be, so much so that you won't *want* to revert back to your old way of living. This is one example of how your focus will shift and change, where material possessions now become less of a priority and having "stuff" no longer matters to you as much as it once did.
- **You Prioritize What Activities You Spend Time On** - Decluttering your life and spending time on activities which are going to be more beneficial for your mind and body are now going to take priority over attending social gatherings or functions that you had no interest in, to begin with. As you start living the life of a true minimalist, if something is not going to align with your values, then they no longer take priority. If a task or commitment is going to take away too much time from doing something that you value, you're going to find it much easier to say no because you now recognize that time is your precious and most valuable resource. The minimalist mindset teaches you how to be intentional with how you're spending and investing your time, and your priorities are going to shift as a result of that.
- **You No Longer Equate Happiness with Objects** - The reason why minimalists are happier than so many others even though they live with less is that their mindset has shifted to where they no longer equate their happiness with objects. They longer believe that having stuff is going to be the reason for their happiness, and therefore, they don't base their happiness on that any longer. They realize that true happiness comes from the relationships they have in their life, or spending their time in activities which fuel their passion and align with what they value the most. This is how they find joy in living a simple life.
- **You Realize That You Don't Need to "Own" Things to Enjoy Them** - Another big shift in your mindset that is going to result from minimalism is the notion that you need to "own" something before you can enjoy them. That was a big part of why you ended up with more things than you should because you *thought* you needed all of it to indulge in the things that you enjoy. Minimalists realize that this is no longer true. They don't need to

own exercise equipment to still benefit from it, because there are plenty of other alternatives like running outdoors, working out in groups at the park, or even downloading workout apps to follow along with. They realize that they don't need to own the latest car model to get where they want to go, because there are always alternatives like carpooling, riding a bike or taking public transport. Minimalism shifts your mindset from thinking *what do I need to buy to do this* to *what alternatives do I have if I don't own this?*

- **You Are Going to Be Aware of Your Time** - You may not have given much thought to how you were spending your time pre minimalism, which made it easy for the minutes and hours to just slip by. Without realizing it, several hours and past and you're left wondering where did the time go. As you remove all the distractions that once crowded your life, you'll come to an awareness that time is your most valuable resource. From this point on, you're going to be acutely aware of just how you're spending your time. Are you spending more time than you should be investing in relationships that you shouldn't? Do you spend far too much of your time online in an unproductive manner? The deeper you go into your journey as a minimalist, the more importance you are going to place on doing things that benefit you, and if something isn't beneficial, then you won't be inclined to waste as much time on it anymore as you once did.

- **Fear No Longer Controls Your Mindset** - The fear of being deprived and living in scarcity that you were once so afraid of is no longer going to be what controls your mind. Once you have embraced minimalism and rid yourself of the "just in case" mentality, you will realize that all those fears which you were holding onto in reality had no basis at all. You will realize that there was nothing to fear because there are always solutions to every problem. In the event that you do find yourself without an item that you need, you now know that it's okay because you do have options to choose from. You could borrow what you need, or make do with what you have if it is good enough and fits in with what you need at the time. Minimalism will shift your mindset to lose the belief that you must hold onto a whole bunch of things which you may or may not use because of the "just in case" factor and instead, teach you to get creative with your solutions because you will realize there is no value in holding onto something that you're hardly ever, or never, going to use.

- **You Are Going to Rediscover Yourself** - When the material possessions are no longer around to serve as a crutch that is distracting you, only then will you be able to take a long, hard look at yourself as you reassess your life. It is only through getting rid of all the things that do not matter that you start to see clearly for the first time in a long time, what does matter. In doing so, you're going to reconnect with yourself and rediscover things about yourself that you may have forgotten for a very long time because you were so distracted and couldn't see that it was right there in front of you.

As with everything else, a gradual shift in your mindset as you immerse yourself into the minimalist lifestyle is a change that is going to happen over time. The best thing you can do is to let go of your old thought patterns and let this change happen gradually on its own. Don't resist it, don't try to fight it off, but rather embrace it just as you are embracing this new lifestyle.

CHAPTER 7
Goal Setting

Deciding to make a change in your life is a step in the right direction. Maintaining though is the next part of the journey that needs working on. How do you maintain this new lifestyle that you have committed yourself to? By setting goals and avoiding mistakes, which is what we will be exploring in this chapter.

What Is a Goal?

If you've got a desire and a vision to achieve something, a goal is what's going to help turn that vision into a reality. The goal is what fuels you to put in the necessary effort required to turn that desire you have from a vision that only exists in your mind into something tangible that becomes part of your achievement. For example, if you have always envisioned living a much happier, simpler life with less stress and clutter filling up your environment, the life of a minimalist, then having goals is how you take the necessary steps towards making that vision happen. Goals push you towards taking action because they require you to make plans, and these plans need a commitment from you, calling for you to stick to these plans and see them through until the end. It's like making a promise to yourself that you need to keep.

Goals are reminders as to why you got started in the first place, and these reminders are going to be the very thing that helps you stay on track and keep moving forward. Why did you want to become a minimalist? What outcome do you hope to achieve by choosing to live this kind of life? What is your long-term and short-term vision that you're hoping to see manifest by taking the necessary steps and embracing minimalism? These are all the things you would have thought about before embarking on this life-changing process, but without the necessary action steps motivating you to get started and get moving, there's nothing concrete for you to focus on. Without a focal point, the chances of you losing sight of why you started in the first place are much higher, and when you've forgotten your 'why', it becomes much easier to give up and revert back to your old ways.

Setting goals for yourself will give you perspective and help shape the next few decisions that you make from this point moving forward. Every decision will affect your life in one way or another, no matter how small or insignificant we think that decision may be. Buying a candy bar, for example, may seem like a tiny decision, but that one decision could cause you to deviate from the weekly budget that you have set for yourself, resulting in a slight overspend for the week. *Every* decision is going to matter, even more so when it comes to the big choices you have to make, such as what items you need to remove from your life, or what relationships you will now choose to invest less time in.

Can Goals *Really* Make a Difference in My Life as A Minimalist?

Yes, it can. Especially if you are new to this process and just starting to discover what life as a minimalist is going to be all about. Goals make a difference because it forces you to think about what's important in your life, what it is you value, and it is going to help you live this new life with a greater sense of purpose. Pre minimalism, you may have spent a lot of time wondering what you're doing with your life, feeling unhappy, disgruntled and perhaps even a little lost because you forgot your sense of purpose along the way. You wanted to get more out of your life, but you did not know how to do it or what needed to be changed. That's because you had no goals to focus on, nothing guiding you down the path that you needed to go. Goals can change all of that.

A goal is going to help you make the decluttering process *significantly* easier. When you set goals for yourself before you begin, having them by your side as you start to remove the excess stuff that you no longer need will make the decision process move much swifter. When you find yourself holding onto one of your items and staring at it for an awfully long time, wondering if you should toss or keep, take a look at your goals again. If this item isn't in line with the goals that you have set for yourself, then there is only one decision to be made. Toss, done and moving onto the next item. See how much more efficient the process can be? Compare that to if you didn't have a goal to focus on. You could spend hours pondering over whether you should get rid of an item or not, going back and forth for days even because you can't quite make up your mind. All of this is precious time which could be used more productively, and goals are here to help speed things along.

Where and How Do I Get Started Setting Goals as a Minimalist?

That's the question that a lot of new minimalists will often ask. In the interest of simplifying and streamlining their lives to make it more efficient through minimalism, *how do you get started creating efficient goals that fit in with this new life?*
As with everything else in minimalism, you want to try and keep your goals simple too. After all, the whole reason you chose to begin this new lifestyle in the first place was that you wanted to step away from your old life where too much was happening and causing you to feel overstressed, overworked and overwhelmed. Therefore, it makes sense to keep your goals within the similar theme of this whole new approach, and the

simpler it is, the easier it will be for you to create habits that are likely to stick.

- **Step 1: Start by Identifying the Goals and How It Fits in With Your Lifestyle.** The beginning of any new life change is where most people find themselves struggling. Identifying your goals in this stage will be key because it will help you prepare for what's ahead, and they kind of goals that you set will either help you or hinder you in your attempts to live like a minimalist. With each goal that you set, think about how it is going to interact with your life and why it would be a good fit. It is important that you be able to answer the question very clearly and definitively because you must know the reason why you are setting this goal. If you are in doubt, then it might not be a goal that is necessary right for you and this change that you're about to go through. To make real progress, you need to think long and hard about what you want your future to look like moving forward. Do you want to live a life where you feel free, happy and healthy, no longer consumed by the desire to constantly compare yourself to others? If yes, how is the goal that you just wrote down going to interact with this vision and make it a reality? Start thinking about the big picture and how to use goals as a tool towards achieving your desired outcome.
- **Step 2: Observe What's Holding You Back.** Of course, this isn't going to be the first time in your life that you would have attempted to set goals for yourself. Most people start every new year with goals and resolutions of what they want to achieve by the time the year reaches an end. Some are successful at making those goals come true, while others are not as successful as the enthusiasm from the start of the new year starts to die down and fade away once they go back to the daily grind of life. Here's where you need to do a little bit of self-reflection, and look back at the past goals you have tried to set but never quite carried out. What factors contributed to this and kept you from turning those goals into reality? What was holding you back? What could you have done differently to change that? The self-reflection part of the process is important because you don't want to be making these same mistakes as you try to set new goals for yourself as a minimalist. Remember, this lifestyle is going to be a *big* change and completely different from the life that you are currently living now. It's a big commitment, and the last thing you want is to get halfway through the process and abandon it. Reassessing what stopped you from carrying out goals in the past will help you confront anything that you might have been afraid of. Perhaps you were worried about the change, or you may not have been ready to get out of your comfort zone just yet.

- **Step 3: Start to Visualize Your Success.** Visualization is the part of goal setting that often gets overlooked, but it is just as necessary as being very clear from the beginning about what your goals are. You must be able to visualize your success with great clarity, see your goals manifest in your life in great detail. Try to even visualize what success is going to feel like for you. The more details you can put into your visualization exercise, the better because it gives you a very clear mental picture of what you should be working towards. It also helps you give your goals deeper thought about how it is going to impact and interact with the lifestyle that you have now chosen for yourself. This is going to be closely connected with Step 1, where you need to start thinking about the bigger picture. Dream about what your life would look like as a minimalist, what your home is going to look like with just the bare essentials, and what life is going to feel like with fewer relationships and commitments cluttering your social calendar. Being able to visualize helps to create a sense of calm, and when you're happy with the vision you see in your mind, you'll be excited and eager to start living the life that you see. The more you visualize, the more attainable your goals will seem to be.
- **Step 4: Making an Action Plan** - Action plan is a must when you are setting goals for yourself. An action plan helps to break down that goal into smaller, more doable tasks that you can work on one by one, setting deadlines for each task even. For instance, if your goal was to have your study area at home cleared out by the end of the week, make an action plan to spend 10-15 minutes over the next 7-days sorting through the items and decluttering anything that you don't need anymore. By the time you reach the end of the week, you would have finished your goal without even realizing it. Without a proper action plan in place, achieving goals can often feel like a struggle, because you don't know where to begin or where you should even start. Minimalism is all about simplifying your life, and that includes the goals that you set for yourself. Have a goal, and break it down into smaller, simpler, action steps that seem far less overwhelming and much easier to start working on.

The Minimalist's Guide to Goal Setting Strategies

Now that you know where to begin with setting out your goals, the next step is to look at the strategies to keep your goals simple. *Minimal.*
- **Start with No More Than 3 Goals** - Always keep in mind that your aim right now is to go for simplicity and avoid clutter. Which means you're going to want to avoid having too many things on

your plate at any given time, including goals. To successfully carry out your goals as a minimalist, aim to have no more than 3 goals that you're working on at any given time. Limiting the goals that you can choose to focus on has the added advantage of making you more mindful towards the kind of goals you are selecting to work on. Since you can only pick 3 at a time and finish those before you move onto newer goals, you really want to make those goals count, so your time and effort does not go to waste. Time is always going to be your most valuable resource, never forget that, so be very selective about how you choose to spend your time. A good tip would be to make your goals inspiring enough that you get excited just thinking about them, so you look forward to the change instead of being hesitant or worried about it. A goal should be so exciting that you can't wait to get started on it and motivated you enough that you want to push through the challenging parts.

- **Manage Your Expectations** - Setting reasonable expectations for your goals is important to avoid disappointments. Often we get carried away setting goals and we can't wait to see the outcome that when it takes longer than expected to achieve, we find ourselves feeling discouraged or disappointed. Setting reasonable expectations is how you avoid falling into that cycle which may cause you to feel demotivated and perhaps even want to give up because you think it's not working out quite like you hoped. Be patient; some things take time, especially big things like making an entire lifestyle change. It is okay to have goals with deadlines attached to them but make those deadlines reasonable.
- **Shift Your Focus** - Instead of thinking too much about the outcome, why not shift your focus towards the process instead? In the wise words of Ralph Waldo Emerson, *it is not the destination that matters, but the journey instead*. And Emerson was right. You're about to embark on a new and exciting journey, something you have never done before. Yes, there are outcomes that you hope to achieve at the end of it, but avoid being so focused on the outcome that you lose sight of the journey that you're taking to get you there. The little habits, the positive changes for the better, the improvements that you're going to feel both physically and mentally are all part of this journey, and if you're too focused on just the outcome, you miss out on these little moments that also matter just as much.
- **Spread Out Your Tasks** - Trying to do everything all at once is how you end up overstretching yourself. Understandably, you want to get the clearing out portion of the process over and done with as soon as possible so you can get to the part where you start to enjoy your newfound clutter-free life, but trying to do too much

too soon will only exhaust yourself. You need to give yourself time to accomplish your tasks and your goals, which is why you needed to set those reasonable expectations in the first place. Depending on the size of your home, clearing it out in a day or two is not going to be possible, unless you've got a lot of free time on your hands and several people to help you. Give yourself a couple of weeks to declutter your home, tackling different sections at a time and making it a goal to finish one section before moving onto the next. This will help prevent you from feeling too stressed or worried that you're not meeting your goal deadlines. Use your time wisely and it will not be wasted, *and* you will still get things done without feeling the pressure.

Common Minimalist Mistakes to Avoid

When you're new at anything, mistakes along the way are to be expected. This includes when you're starting out your new life as a minimalist. Mistakes, however, are sometimes the best way for you to learn, so don't be too hard on yourself if it happens. The best way to minimize the mistakes that occur is to prepare beforehand by arming yourself with the knowledge about what these mistakes are so you can avoid them when the time comes.

- **Mistake #1: Putting Pressure on Yourself to Be Perfect** - Minimalism is not about perfection, and if you are expecting it to be, you're only putting unnecessary pressure on yourself to achieve an unattainable concept. Minimalism is not meant to be a process that is going to stress you out, or something that you're going to regret later on. It shouldn't be a process that is forcing you to constantly think about how and what you could do better. Minimalism is not about pursuing perfection; it is about pursuing happiness and balance in your life once again. Life is never perfect, and that is what makes living each day so exciting.
- **Mistake #2: Being Too Strict with Yourself** - Minimalism is not a binary choice, and that is one mistake that often gets made. Minimalism can be what you want it to be. You can still be minimal while living in a big home if it works for you, and there is certainly no rule that says you need to toss out almost everything that you own before you can be considered a true minimalist. Some minimalists have more possessions than others, but that doesn't make them any less of a minimalist. This lifestyle is going to be entirely personal and tailored to suit what works best for you, so you don't have to be too strict on yourself. If there's an aspect of minimalism that doesn't work well for you, you can choose to adapt and modify it into something that does work. No need to make yourself miserable over the process, because this is meant to be a change for the better, not worse.

- **Mistake #3: Getting Rid of Stuff Doesn't Mean You Can Buy More Stuff** - Another rookie mistake which often gets made is the idea that by decluttering the old stuff from our lives, we can buy new stuff because we now have more space. That is not what minimalism is about. You need to now learn to live with less and live with only what's important, that's the whole point. Decluttering is not a window of opportunity to go out and buy more new stuff just because you have all this extra space in your home. It is okay to have empty spaces around your home, not every nook and cranny needs to be crammed full of stuff.
- **Mistake #4: Thinking That Being a Minimalist Means You Will Automatically Be Happy** - You will, but not in the way that you think. Getting rid of the clutter in your home and your life does not equal automatic happiness, and thinking that way will only lead to disappointment. Minimalism doesn't work like that. Material possessions won't make you feel happy and fulfilled the way that you hoped, but neither will tossing everything out. Happiness is something that comes from within, and it's not about how much or how little you have. Minimalism teaches you to be *content* with what you have and to find happiness in the things that matter more than material goods. For true happiness to exist within you, you need to be happy with who you are and what you already have and to stop looking externally for a solution.
- **Mistake #5: Trying to Avoid Making Purchases Altogether** - Minimalism is not an extreme, and if you genuinely have a need for something, you shouldn't restrict yourself from buying it. Minimalists shop less, but they still do shop and buy the things that they need to survive. It's not that they have now decided to avoid shopping altogether, they have just changed the way that they now make purchases based on their priorities.
- **Mistake #6: Feeling Obligated to Keep Certain Items** - There's no real need for you to keep something around if it isn't adding value to your life. If you're using that approach towards decluttering, you're going to still be holding onto a lot of unnecessary items, which then defeats the purpose of minimalism in the first place.
- **Mistake #7: Thinking Minimalism Is Going to Fix Your Problems** - Minimalism is not a quick fix for happiness, and it is not a band-aid or magic formula that is going to make all your problems just go away. Going into minimalism thinking that it is going to help fix the problems you have in your life is only going to leave you feeling disappointed. The problems will still be there until you do something to fix it. Minimalism is meant to make life easier for you by removing the clutter and distractions, but it

won't remove the problems, and doing it because that's the outcome you're hoping more means you're doing it for all the wrong reasons.
- **Mistake #8: Waiting for the "Right Time" Before You Get Started -** There will never be a "right time" or "perfect time" to get started, and if you're always going to be waiting on that before you make a change, you're going to be waiting for a very long time. Perhaps even not going through it at all. You need to make it the "right time" for yourself based on your schedule, and just start by putting one foot in front of the other until you slowly gain momentum. Waiting for things to be perfect before getting started is how a lot of people let opportunities in life pass them by because they didn't seize the moment. There will never be a right time; it is up to you to *make the time right.*

CHAPTER 8
Success Tips For Your New Way Of Life

Now that you have learned about the minimalist way of life and how it benefits you, it is time to start putting a plan in place. Below is a step-by-step guide to help you embark on your journey towards minimalism.

Step 1: Set a vision

Setting a vision and a plan is important because you don't want to find yourself falling back into your old habits. As Sue Grafton puts it, *"Ideas are easy. It's the execution of ideas that really separates the sheep from the goats."*

Try to envision what your life would be like when you apply this lifestyle and determine in your mind that this is really what you want to happen. Always start with the 'why.' Perhaps you intend to declutter to ensure you are able to focus on the important things in life. Perhaps, you are choosing this lifestyle to save money. Whatever it is, determining your 'why' is important because this is what you will fall back on every time you hit a roadblock.

After considering the 'why,' you need to think about your 'how.' How do you envision yourself transitioning into this lifestyle? Some people prefer to do this area by area, and some prefer to go full-on, cold turkey. This is ultimately your choice. Choose something that works best for you and that you think is achievable. Try not to set too high an expectation that will discourage you when you are not able to cultivate the habit.

Lastly, think about what you are trying to achieve as a minimalist. Set measurable goals that will encourage you on your journey, and consistently act as a reminder of why you have chosen this life. It could be as simple as saving a few hundred bucks a month to, seeing how your home is transformed room by room. It could also come in the form of time, where you have an extra hour a day to spend on your hobbies.

Step 2: Change your perspective

In order to change your lifestyle, your mindset has to change first. A minimalist mindset is simple - everything fits, and almost everything is black and white. Set rules to help you make decisions, and commit to them. If there are things that you do on a daily basis, try to develop a routine that will help you accomplish these activities with minimal effort and time as possible. Old ways may feel comfortable, but they may not be the most effective.

Another example of shifting your mindset would be to choose what you want to keep instead of what you want to get rid of. Many people feel like they have to discard a lot of things when they choose to live as a minimalist, but a change of perspective would help, when you think about what you should keep instead if helps you take on a more positive perspective and reduces stress of being separated from your beloved things.

Step 3: Simplify

Decluttering your mind is also a part of being a minimalist. Minimalist living is simplifying your life also through the way you think. In your process of eliminating things, ask yourself if it is possible for you to discard it. You are allowed to be honest with yourself. How far can you go in cutting these certain things from your life?

The next question you can ask is, "Can I delegate it?" People tend not only to hoard things but tasks as well. Sometimes, we take ownership of something and continue to feel responsible for it although our roles have progressed. Assess if this kind of 'work' should still be your responsibility. If not, delegate.

Lastly, if there is something that is not worth your time, outsource help. Hire someone else to do the job so you can clear your head and spend time to focus on something more important. Time is money, and if you feel that your time is worth more than what you can pay someone else to do, hire help.

Step 4: Apply to all areas

Unless all areas of your life are decluttered, you are not considered a minimalist. Physical, mental and emotional are almost always aligned. Therefore, you can start getting rid of physical clutter first before trying to declutter every other part of your life. We will explore more later in the chapter, but below is the list of areas you can start with.

Areas to declutter

Physical

The most obvious way to determine whether you have a problem with hoarding is to look into your living space, but being able to identify it also means it is the easiest to declutter and the first place you should look into when embarking on your minimalist way of life. The most common physical spaces to declutter is your wardrobe, the bedroom, your office and the kitchen.

The wardrobe is the most common area where people accumulate access. Keep what you love and donate the rest. A bedroom is for sleep, and where your body recuperates from your day. So, get rid of disruptive noises, namely the television. Hint, getting rid of the television declutters two areas of your life, the bedroom, and your mind. In your office, try to arrange your things in binders instead of piling it on.

Below are some tips on how you can declutter these physical areas in your home:

The closet

1. The first thing you can do is to first decide how much you really need. Honestly, you only need a few items for each occasion and putting a number to each category can help you decide whether to keep or bin your clothing items.
2. Get rid of any clothing item that is damaged. If it is torn or has huge holes, it's time to let it go.
3. If you haven't worn it in over a year, chances are you won't be wearing it ever again. Put it in the 'donate pile.'
4. Choose the items you absolutely love, or cannot live without. Tally it with the number of clothes that you need, and see if you have more to spare. If not, get rid of the rest.
5. You only need enough undergarments to last you for the week. Those really old and worn-out ones that are comfy but you cannot bring yourself to wear belong in the 'throw bin.'
6. Decide what shoes you really need and keep the ones that you wear often. Shoes do not last long in the closet and they deteriorate quickly if not worn - ironically. Ideally, keep those that are versatile and can be worn with any clothing item.

The kitchen

1. The most obvious thing to clear out of the kitchen are expired goods. This is not only for the minimalists but for those who want to avoid visiting the emergency room. You'd be surprised how many homes have expired goods in their fridge or cabinets
2. Throw away anything that is broken. This can range from dishes to appliances. If it is chipped, cracked or unusable for over a year, it's time to throw it away.
3. Like in the previous exercise with your closet, determine how many items are essential to your kitchen, and donate or bin the rest.
4. One of the common guidelines you can use is to keep 1 mug for each person living in your home, and a few more extra in case you have visitors.
5. If you have any appliances that are not in use or duplicates of necessities like measuring cups or blenders, donate or sell them.

6. Invest in high-quality items. A good stainless steel or heavy-duty cast-iron skillet will serve you well for a long time. This can also prevent you from spending more.

The living room

1. Go digital. Put all your movies and music that are still in its cases to your computer. This way, you can get rid of its plastic cases and recycle them. This saves you a ton of space in your living room.
2. Donate books that you no longer read. It is understandable that books may be sentimental to some people. However, if they are not important to you and you don't intend to read them anymore, donate or sell them. You can also participate in book exchanges. Better yet, visit your local library to read and clear out all your books.
3. Get rid of things that you don't use, need or like. Most living rooms are filled with souvenirs, toys or packaging that we thought were nice some time ago. If they aren't functional, beneficial or spark joy, get rid of them.
4. Throw away or donate your throw pillows. Throw pillows were a thing some time ago (maybe they are still a novelty in some households), but they take up a lot of space and most of them end up not being used. Donate pillows that you no longer need in your home.
5. If you have kids, and they have a mountain of toys, use the same guide as the above. Throw away those that are broken, no longer spark joy, and think about how much your children actually need. Most kids outgrow their toys. If they do not age appropriate, donate them.

The bathroom

1. Some people collect toiletries from their travel and most of them are kept unused for a long time. Use whatever you have before buying more. Make it a point to finish using your current toiletries before being tempted to buy a different brand or range.
2. Go through your medicine cabinet and check the labels. If they are expired, throw them out. Different countries have different regulations on how to dispose of medicines. Be sure to check yours before disposing of any drugs.
3. Donate all unused towels. Keep a few extra and donate the rest. Towels last you a long time and it'll be long until you need a new one.

4. You only need one of each of your appliances like hair dryers, curling irons, shavers, or straightening irons. If you have extra, donate them.
5. Ideally, your powder makeup should only last you up to 2 years, and your lipsticks a year. If you have some that are older than that, throw them away.

The above discussed are tips on how to declutter the physical spaces in your home. It may not apply to you in entirety but rest assured that a little goes a long way. Next, we will look into minimizing digital and mental clutter.

Digital

One of the most easily gathered, but less obvious clutter in our lives are digital. Try to minimize time on the phone, or turn off notifications at times where you intend to rest. Sometimes, unfollowing or unfriending unnecessary people on our social media does wonders for us mentally.

On your computers, organize your desktop and delete files that are no longer in use. Sometimes, closing tabs and programs that you are not actively using can also clear your mind and allow you to focus on what you need to be doing.

You can also choose to make use of certain websites that allow you to access content and stream online instead of downloading. While it may be impossible to totally disengage from everything digital, doing a digital or social media fast once a while will help you be more aware of the present and your surroundings.

Below are some things you can begin doing to declutter digitally:

Unsubscribe from emails that you don't read

Unsubscribing from newsletters or notifications from companies or brands that we don't need will not only reduce digital clutter but also mental clutter. We don't need to be flooded with promotions that don't apply to us, or information that is irrelevant to us. When you feel that they are relevant again, you can always re-subscribe.

Organize and clear your email inbox

Most of us have unread emails that date back for years. Clear them out and try to organize your emails by sender or by categorizing your folders.

Organize and clean up your Desktop

Placing files on your desktop for easy access is always tempting. However, whenever you turn on your computer and the first thing you see is clutter, the 'easy access' can in time, turn into disruptive excess. Organize files in folders instead and delete the ones you no longer need.

Uninstall software that you don't use

If you no longer need a particular software, uninstall it to clear up space in your computer. This also helps you find programs that you actually need easily.

Delete unused files

There is no argument here. If you no longer need it, delete it to make room for what you actually need.

Turn off unimportant notifications on your mobile

Unsolicited notifications can distract you from the present, drain your mental energy and also your batteries. Take 2 minutes to turn off unimportant notifications from applications that you use rarely.

Clean your browser by deleting cookies, plugins or cache

Although the intention for cookies and cache is to store information to help you load pages faster, they can quickly add up act adversely. It is important to clear out cookies and cache to clear up space and save computing power.

Organize your files in folders

It is a given that organizing your files in folders will ensure easy access. You will also save time looking for the particular files.

Mental

Sometimes, we unintentionally collect mental clutter by setting unnecessary expectations on ourselves based on what others are doing. For instance, the perception that you absolutely have to own your own home is a mental burden that you may not need. If it is currently too far-fetched or not in your capabilities, then rent and be okay with it. There is no point putting unnecessary pressure on yourself.

Scheduling regular meditation or 'me time' is vital to your mental health. It allows you to reflect, identify unproductive thoughts and declutter. This will result in mental clarity and better ability to focus on the important aspects of your life.

One of the most common mental stressors for people is money. Worrying about money is one of the major sources of migraines and headaches. If you have a debt, focus on paying it off before setting any other financial commitments or goals. Declutter your financial ins and outs, and try to set simple goals like spending less than you earn, or saving up to 20% of your salary each month. The less time you spend worrying about money is more time spent on things that you enjoy.

Some mind clutter is also often related to our past. We tend to think about the mistakes we've made, opportunities we didn't take and those who have hurt us. Take time to address these feelings, deal with them and let them go. If you can fix them, do it. If not, best to forgive yourself, forgive those who have hurt you and move on.

One of the things therapists encourage patients to do is to write their thoughts and feelings down. They may or may not be reasonable or rational, but writing them down can help clear its recurrence in your mind and decreases your mental burden. Putting it down on paper helps you visualize your thoughts and you can begin to make sense of them. At the end of it, you can make an informed decision of whether or not to keep these thoughts or give them a place in your mind.

Sustaining Your Minimalistic Lifestyle

Now that you have a plan and are ready to set things in motion, you need to ensure you're in for the long haul. Remember that it takes time to get into the groove of a lifestyle change and you will need to be prepared to tackle minor discouragements and setbacks along the way and ensure that you stay on track.

As long as you are prepared with a system in place, you should have no problem sustaining your minimalistic lifestyle. Below are a few rules you can use as guidelines when setting your sustainability system.

90 Days Rule

When clearing out your spaces, look at each item and think about whether you have used it in the last 90 days. If you haven't, it is unlikely that you will use them again. Choose to bin or donate them. If you can set a benchmark of fewer days, the better.

Weekly Reflection

Review your progress and run a health check on how you're doing as a minimalist. It is always good to reflect, declutter, and refocus on your priorities. The more often you reflect, the less likely you are to find clutter; be it physical, mental or digital. This also ensures that you are running on a clear focus on priorities.

Quality vs Quantity

Choose to buy high-quality things that last you for a longer time, compared to quantity. This will reduce the need to eliminate things in your life and actually save you more money in the long run. It also saves you the time you spend repairing something that often breaks or needs more maintenance than a low-quality one.

When it comes to food, whole food is better than processed. Invest time cooking and save money buying fresh instead of processed and packaged foods. This also contributes to better and stronger immune system.

Tradeoff

Whenever you decide to buy a new item, you have to swap and get rid of the item that you already have. But before you decide to buy something, question whether you need it. If you already have something that functions the same, resist!

Be flexible

Sometimes along the way, you discover that the plans or systems you put in place may not suit your needs or goals. It is okay to recalibrate and reset new plans or goals. This is why constant reflection is needed. A few changes could take place before you finally find something that you are comfortable with.

One step at a time

Trying to declutter your entire home at one go is not the best idea. Try to set a timeline to clear out specific areas in your house first, and see how well you do. Attempting too much at the beginning could cause massive discouragement and fallout. You could start with one room and arrange items into three (3) piles: Keep, Throw or Donate.

Create a schedule

When planning to sustain your lifestyle, it is important to think about scheduling regular clear-outs. It's one thing to clear things out, and another thing to *keep* things out. To ensure that the clutter does not creep its way back in, it's important to set time for regular review of the items in your home.

Travel Light

The two main rules that minimalists abide by when travelling is to bring a small bag and differentiating between needs and wants. Try not to bring a big bag during travel unless you want to fill it up. This could either mean bringing excess things for travel or bringing home more than what you intend to.

Next, think about where you're going and what are the essentials. For instance, if you're going to the beach, you need flip flops, bathing suits, sunglasses and shorts. Wants include extra dresses, inflatables, costume jewelry and heels.

Redesign your home

This doesn't mean major renovation, but it could be rearranging furniture and clearing out things that are merely decorative, and collect dust over time. If you find ornaments or souvenirs that have years of dust resting over it, it's time to let them go.

Designing a home that is simple and clean can help you feel calm and better sustain the minimalist lifestyle. You are less likely to continue accumulating things you don't need.

Cook with less

As mentioned earlier, whole foods are always better. You can whip up a good meal with ten ingredients or less, saving you more money and cutting down on waste created by the packaging of the processed foods. Better yet, plan your meals and have a shopping list, so you don't come home from the supermarket with extra things you bought on impulse.

Cultivate edifying hobbies

Often times, people end up spending money on things that don't edify them or add to their growth. Think about what you enjoy doing and fill your time with useful hobbies that will grow your talents or skills, or something that you actually enjoy doing. If you have to invest your time on something, it better be for something that's good for you.

If the hobbies are free, that's a bonus. Free hobbies will help you live a more minimal life. Hobbies like outdoor sports like yoga or running helps you clear your mind, maintain wellness and also accumulate fewer things.

Be grateful

Lastly, in your reflection, remember to be thankful for the things that you have. Be thankful for the luxury of being able to travel, donating excess, spend time with your hobbies and being able to create a clean space for you and your mind.

Conclusion

In your journey towards minimalism, always remember your end goal and be kind to yourself. As mentioned earlier, a lifestyle change takes time. Remember your purpose and do what works best for you in order to achieve it.

Conclusion

Thank for making it through to the end of this book, let's hope it was informative and able to provide you with all of the tools you need to achieve your goals whatever they may be.

This is an exciting journey you're about to embark on, and hopefully, you're just as eager to get started after reading through the chapters of this book. The transition into the lifestyle of a minimalist can be a deeply fulfilling experience. It may be daunting to think about living life with just the bare necessities and only a few worldly possessions to your name, but once you fully immerse yourself into the experience, you will wonder why it took you so long to get started in the first place.

This is going to be a unique experience for each and every one of you, but the ultimate goal is going to be the same - *to declutter your life, find your focus again, that happiness cannot be found in material goods and rearrange your priorities to remind yourself about what's truly important in life.* Rearranging your life is going to put so many things into perspective, and it is up to you to use this newfound focus and hopefully extra time on your hands in a more productive manner. Go after the goals you have been pushing aside for so long, reconnect with old friends and strengthen existing relationships, commit to your health, your passions and explore new interests you've never had the opportunity to before. The world is yours for the taking; all you have to do is to start living your life the way that it was meant to be lived.

No more will you have to be a slave to consumerism; this is the start of a brand-new beginning. Take each day as it comes and open your heart and your mind to new possibilities as you go forth and begin your minimalist lifestyle.

Finally, if you found this book useful in any way, a review on Amazon is always appreciated!

DESCRIPTION

How would you like to live a life that is *simple*?
How would you like to live a life that is *free?*
Free from the stress, worries and anxieties that plague most of us each day as we spend countless hours, day in and day out, trying to keep up with the never-ending demands of a materialistic lifestyle? Free from the constraints of living paycheck to paycheck? Free from the mess and clutter that surrounds your home to a point you don't know where certain items are kept anymore?
How would you like to live a life that is lighter, happier and more focused on the things that matter most in life? Relationships, life experiences, passion, joy, happiness and all these priceless parts of life you somehow forgot about along the way?
All that you long for can be yours, and all it takes is one change in your life — the change from becoming a *consumerist* to a *minimalist*.
Did you know that on average, almost all of us own more than what we actually need to survive? And more often than not, this excess of 'stuff' is unnecessary. How many items have you purchased in the past thinking that you need them, only to find that you never use them? How many items do you have around your home that you forgot you even purchased? This accumulation of items is not doing you any favors, and in fact, all you're doing is cluttering up your home and adding more mess onto your already busy, hectic life. You're spending hard earned money which you could put to much better use on things that you don't even necessarily need.
It is for those very reasons and more that minimalism is now gaining popularity as people start to realize *you know what? I don't need all this stuff at all.*
Minimalist Lifestyle: How to Become a Minimalist, Declutter Your Life and Develop Minimalism Habits & Mindsets to Worry Less and Live More is step-by-step guide that will show you how to transition from the life that you know, into the life of a minimalist with insightful advice and helpful strategies that are easy to follow and apply. Explore:
- What it means to live life as a minimalist
- The rules of living with less
- How to minimize other aspects of your life (finances, health, relationships and more)
- What it takes to make the mindset shift
- Why it is important to set goals for yourself as you begin this new lifestyle
- *And more...*

Start your simple, stress-free approach to living today with all the tools that you need to help you get started off on the right foot from Day 1. Isn't it about time that you started to worry less and live more?

www.ingramcontent.com/pod-product-compliance
Lightning Source LLC
Chambersburg PA
CBHW071407070526
44578CB00002B/511